JOHN CALVIN
and the Calvinistic Tradition

plus penetrante que

La parolle de Dieu est vive & efficace, &

tout glaiue à deux trenchans. Ebrieux 4.

I G

Men of Wisdom

JOHN CALVIN
AND THE CALVINISTIC TRADITION

by
ALBERT-MARIE SCHMIDT

Translated by
RONALD WALLACE

NEW YORK
HARPER & BROTHERS

LONDON
LONGMANS

Longmans, Green and Co Ltd
6 & 7 clifford street, london w i
605-611 lonsdale street, melbourne c i
443 lockhart road, hong kong
accra, auckland, ibadan
kingston (jamaica), kuala lumpur
lahore, nairobi, salisbury (rhodesia)
Longmans Southern Africa (Pty) Ltd
thibault house, thibault square, cape town
Longmans, Green and Co Inc
119 west 40th street, new york 18
Longmans, Green and Co
20 cranfield road, toronto 16
Orient Longmans Private Ltd.
calcutta, bombay, madras
delhi, hyderabad, dacca

HARPER AND BROTHERS
49 east 33rd street
new york 16

Library of Congress Catalog Card Number 60–8972

*First published in France
by Editions du Seuil, Paris*

english translation © longmans, green & co ltd 1960

This English edition first published 1960

type set by western printing services ltd., bristol
printed in great britain by lowe and brydone (printers) ltd.

CONTENTS

JOHN CALVIN

PROLOGUE

I have not been so foolish as to try to write a new life of John Calvin. Calvin's over-sensitive modesty made him reticent in revealing himself, and there are many obscure episodes in his career on which it is too difficult a task to throw new light. Nor have I attempted here to prove his greatness and catholicity by giving a complete summary of his teaching. My task rather has been to gather together the various things he told us about himself and his actions, and from these to endeavour to bring out the basic features of a portrait of the man's mind. In doing so my purpose has been not to make my readers mere enthusiastic devotees of the reformer from Picardy, but, rather, to lead them to a recognition of the unchanging relevance of the tasks he undertook, and the pressing urgency of the religious problems which he tried to solve.

Calvin (Portrait in Tronchin collection)

EARLY CHILDHOOD

Everything conspired to make Calvin a great theologian. He was born on 10 July, 1509, at Noyon, a town noted for its many holy places and for the reputed efficacy of its objects of traditional religious veneration. His father, Gérard Cauvin, came from artisan stock and from a family of manual workers. His appointment as registrar for the community left him ample leisure to undertake also the functions of solicitor to the episcopal court, fiscal agent, secretary to the Bishop, and attorney of the Cathedral Chapter. He was a shrewd lawyer who dealt out good advice to his fellow citizens. He was one of the influential men of Noyon. He lived with his family in a pleasant and substantial-looking house.

Gérard Cauvin's ambition was to add lustre to his family name. He felt that the stigma of low birth which attached to his sons could be wiped out only by devoting them either to the legal profession or to the Church. His wife, pious Jeanne le Franc, saw to it that young John Calvin faithfully took part in

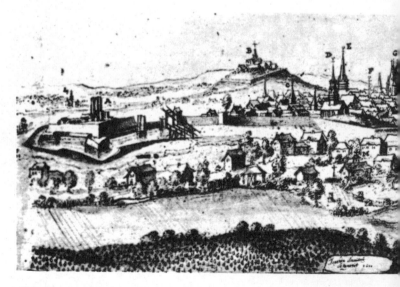

'Noyon, a town noted for its many holy places . . .'

the impressive rites of the religious life of the community, and often took him to Ourscamp Abbey to give veneration to the relics of Saint Anne. Gérard, on the other hand, busied himself in making sure than his son would have influential patrons, and was careful to teach him good manners so that he would be acceptable in the highest society. He was carried away by the refinement and liveliness of his mind and he dreamed of making him an outstanding scholar. 'From the time I was a little child,' writes Calvin, 'my father had destined me to become a theologian.'[1]

Cold, determined, meditative, he entered with zeal upon this way of life which seemed to offer scope for his budding genius. The clergy of Noyon were favourably disposed towards him, encouraged his efforts, and provided him with several benefices while he was still very young. All he needed was some scholastic success and he could be assured of a career in which honours would come easily. Moreover, there was every indication that it was his own diligence which was giving rise to the ambitious hopes that were centred on him.

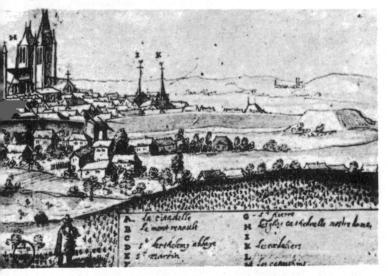

'*A pleasant and substantial-looking house* . . .'

EARLY EDUCATION

It was the done thing amongst the good *bourgeoisie* of Noyon to send their sons to the college of the Capettes. Here Calvin too went as a new boy to learn the rudiments of rhetoric and grammar. He had soon absorbed as much in the way of education as the provincial schoolmasters to whom he had been entrusted could give him. His father managed to send him to Paris in 1523. There he lodged in the home of one of his uncles who was a locksmith. But he did not risk confining himself to such an artisan milieu where he might have lost ground in his studies, and he cultivated the fellowship of the Hangest-Montmors, young noblemen of his own age, the nephews of the Bishop, his father's patron.

Fortune smiled on this austere student of fourteen. In spite of the vexation caused by a tutor whom he found dull and stupid,[2] he matriculated as a non-resident student in the Collège de la Marche, whose buildings adorned the slope of Mont St Geneviève. There he became friendly with one teacher for whom he had a deep respect and whose class he attended for some months: Mathurin Cordier (1479–1564).

This man had scrapped the pomp and circumstance of the university teaching of the day. His one aim was to help his pupils to become what it was in them to be. By a kindly human approach to their minds he sought to bring to birth within them the first exciting stirrings of intellectual life. To him Calvin owed those things which made him outstanding as a writer: a certain taste for picking out and commenting on the examples of morality which are scattered through the old texts, a respect for the cautiousness of wise scholarship, a love for oratorical expression which enables him to refresh his reader at the very moment when he is submitting him to the strain of having to give extra concentration.

ACADEMIC CAREER

But the liberal humanism of Mathurin Cordier was not sufficient preparation for Calvin in view of the ecclesiastical offices which his father was soliciting for him, and in 1524 he became a member of the austere community of the college of Montaigu. In the eyes of the partisans of the new spirit of the age this place stood for everything that violated nature. It had the reputation of ruining the health of its inmates, and of even bringing them to the verge of insanity through the rigours of the inhuman way of life to which they had to submit. In actual fact, in accordance with the rules laid down by the Fleming, Jean Standonck, they formed a voluntary association of youths who sought virtue as well as learning. They were not united by any explicit vow, but they pledged themselves to obey strictly their superiors chosen from among themselves, and to sit no academic examination without express permission from those over them. Undernourished, refusing their bodies the superficial attention necessary for even a minimum of cleanliness, they fasted, they meditated, they imposed a rule of silence on themselves, worked from dawn to nightfall, and submitted meekly to the punishment meted out to them for the slightest carelessness or breach of discipline.

Since he believed that a severe rule of outward life ensured the development of human character, John Calvin accepted the coercion and ill treatment without a murmur. During the five years of his stay at Montaigu he took care not to become involved in the rowdyism of the students of Paris, showed himself amenable to advice from those over him, found real pleasure in yielding himself to the mortifications which they prescribed for him, and decided irrevocably that the Christian life, even if it should be cast under happy earthly circumstances, ought to be characterized by unceasing asceticism.

The professors at Montaigu were under the influence both of their principal, Jean Tempête, and that of Noel Béda (*d.* 1537), dean of the faculty of theology. It was easy for them to convince Calvin of the errors of humanism. They proved to him that the revival of interest in antiquity, far from confirming the Christian conscience, had an enfeebling effect on it. They advised him to take the more positive course of studying the Church Fathers, especially the writings of Augustine of Hippo. He also had to listen to a commentary on the theses of Duns Scotus on the sovereignty of God and on the Eucharist, the aptness of which won his admiration. Finally they showed him the useful subtleties of the philosophy known as nominalist terminism, which is of such ill repute today.

After showing him how human thought can be broken up into its various elements and contained within its natural limits, and how a certain order can be imposed on the free play of ideas, they taught him the art of dialectics. From them he acquired a skill in argument all the more formidable because of his condemnation of everything that savours of intemperance and ecstasy, and his own ability to keep his reason within bounds by repressing the unruly instincts by which it can be carried away.

The Church of Noyon, being informed of his diligence, encouraged him in his zeal, and bestowed on him a new ecclesiastical benefice in 1527. In 1528 he obtained the degree of Master of Arts.

DISQUIETUDE

About this time of his life he allowed a few harmless pleasures to give him relaxation from his work, but only in a very restricted measure. Affable, courteous, vivacious, eloquent, he drew to him the patronage of the learned doctors and the friendship of his equals. Either at Montaigu where the celebrated, fastidiously intelligent John Mair was trying to refute the heresies of Wyclif and Hus, or at the publishing house of Guillaume Cop (*d.* 1532), first physician to the King and a close friend of Erasmus' correspondent Guillaume Budé (1468–1540), Calvin listened to the reformists' and reformers' daring propositions being quoted and possibly disputed. Although the uneasiness they aroused in him was unallayed by his masters' teaching, he did not give way to the temptation of doubting the truth of the strict theological system on which he was being nurtured. He admitted later (1558) that he was at that time 'stubbornly addicted to popish superstitions'.[3] In his admirable address to the Sovereign Judge (1539), he describes the spiritual torment which, out of delicacy, he kept to himself.

> . . . Nor was this apprehension the product of my own inward imagination but it was worked up in me by the doctrines which were then preached everywhere by the teachers and doctors of Christ's people. They indeed preached Thy clemency towards men, but only towards those who made themselves worthy to receive it. And finally they made the righteousness of works of such vital importance that only he was received by grace who could be reconciled to Thee by his own works. All the time they never kept quiet among themselves about our all being miserable sinners who often fall through the weakness of the flesh. And after that, they said that Thy mercy was for all men the common haven of salvation. But to obtain it they held out no other means than that of making satisfaction for our sins. And then such satisfaction was demanded from us; first of all, after having confessed all our sins to a priest we must humbly beseech from him pardon and absolution; secondly, by good works we must wipe out from before Thee the memory of our evil doings; finally, to make up what was still lacking we must add sacrifices and solemn acts of expiation. Then because Thou

wert a stern judge, a strict avenger of iniquity they showed how dreadful Thy presence must be. And because of this they told us to turn for help first of all to the saints that by their intercession Thou mightest be rendered propitious and kind towards us.

And when I had performed all these things in an indifferent way, though I took some small comfort from it, I was still far removed from any assured peace of conscience, for whenever I examined my own self, or lifted my heart up to Thee, a terror so extreme seized me that no expiations or satisfactions could give me any cure. And the more closely I examined myself the more was my conscience tormented by sharp stings so that there was no solace or comfort left to me save that of deluding myself by oblivion.

Still, because nothing better was offered I continued always the course I had begun when, lo, there appeared a very different kind of teaching, not something to lead us away from the Christian profession, but something to bring it back to its true fountainhead, and purging it from all its filth, to restore it to its original purity. But as for me, offended by this novelty, scarcely would I lend my ear to it, and at first I confess I strenuously and boldly resisted. For—since men are naturally obstinate and prejudiced to maintain what they have once received and upheld—it was an agony to confess that all my life long I had been in ignorance and error. And one thing in particular kept me from believing these new teachers; that was, reverence for the Church.[4]

Affable, courteous, vivacious, eloquent . . .

(Calvin as a youth, Hanau Library)

JURISPRUDENCE

Having become somewhat less severe toward himself, Calvin, hoping to overcome the distressing perplexity of his mind, decided that he would strive to acquire the kind of philological skill which his masters at Montaigu looked on as worthless and harmful. At that moment his father took an unforeseen decision and urged him to stop dedicating himself so heroically to the attainment of sacred knowledge.

As he formed the opinion [Calvin notes] that the legal profession usually brings wealth to those who follow it, that hope at once made him change his mind. And that is why I was withdrawn from the study of philosophy and put to the study of the law, and although to obey my father, I strove to apply

myself faithfully, God, however, by His secret providence guided me towards a different path.[5]

Anxious to sit at the feet of the best jurists of his day, he left for Orleans (1528). Although now free from any rules as a student he kept on mortifying his emaciated body. In order to cure it of several different ailments which had struck it down, he cut down his food to a miserable level. This, he claimed, was his method of making his mind more free, and of improving his memory. Silence was for him a kind of intellectual fasting. Therefore he spoke sparingly, and had too much respect for the mystery of communication by speech to deign to indulge in plausible and idle conversation. He had difficulty in overcoming his shyness. Without having sought it, however, he found himself pleasantly popular among the members of his 'nation',

'He set out for Orleans . . .'

the guild which it was compulsory for him to join. He so charmed them by his fine manners, his strength of will, and faultless behaviour that they elected him procurator.

This position imposed on him a certain amount of administrative work which did not, however, prevent him from taking a course of study under the celebrated Pierre de l'Estoile (1480–1537). He admired 'the penetrating power of his mind, his competency, his knowledge of the law,' of which, as he was to write later, 'he is the unchallenged prince of our times'.[6] The mental simplicity of this clever man appealed to Calvin. Here was one scrupulous in his respect for tradition but nevertheless trying to apply the newly invented humanist methods of interpreting and illustrating texts to enrich the traditional findings, without, however, modifying them. It was not just to please his father and to obtain high office that Calvin acquired some knowledge of the law. He hoped to draw from it some of the prin-

'He followed Melchior Wolmar to Bourges . . .

ciples which can help a man to have orderly dealings with his neighbours, and even with a God whose absolute sovereignty he enjoyed defining with expressions borrowed from Roman law.

Besides all this, switching at will from one mood to another, he learned in a few months to read and understand Greek. This success was due to the careful tuition he took from a German humanist, Melchior Wolmar (1497–1561). This man, a zealous Lutheran, undoubtedly urged him to throw in his lot on the side of the Reformation, but Calvin, with a deference that showed the respect in which he held him, was firm in resisting his entreaties. He was sufficiently attached to him, however, to follow him to Bourges where in response to an urgent invitation from Marguerite d'Angoulême (1492–1549), he settled down for a while in 1529. He lived in her house. He concentrated on reading and commenting on the New Testament in its original text, and his spare time was passed in listening to the perform-

André Alçiat, or the art of persuasion

ances of Andrea Alciati (1492–1550)—one whose fame was greater than was deserved. This infatuated Italian looked upon himself as so superior in refinement to his surroundings that he felt like an exile in the bosom of a barbaric people. He used to select some of the ticklish juridical problems, deliberately make them more complicated than need be, and made all this the occasion for racy set-speeches, delivered with studied ease, which caused his refined audience to praise and acclaim him. After hearing him Calvin realized, even better than from Mathurin Cordier's learned lectures, that the main elements in the art of speaking persuasively are elegance, the right choice of words, and harmony in style. But he detested the boasting, the stuff and nonsense, the empty and frivolous words of this braggart from beyond the Alps, and this served to make him feel even more deeply his professed admiration for the conscience and strict respect for truth of the great Pierre de l'Estoile, whom right to the end of his life he considered one of the most formative influences in his thinking.

LANGUAGE STUDY

If Melchior Wolmar did not succeed in altering Calvin's rather regretful attachment to the Roman Church, he at least tried to make him aware of the latent power of his own genius. He tried to make him see that he would never find lasting satisfaction by quibbling about trivialities, and that theology alone could enable him to find a unifying order and purpose in the various branches of knowledge which he had already explored. Calvin could not make up his mind. Religious controversy was distasteful to one so unassuming. He would rather have lived the peaceful life of a learned Christian recluse. But by this time he had completed all his preparation for his *licence ès lois* which he obtained probably in 1530.

By now his interest and curiosity had been already stirred by reading some of Luther's treatises and writings. But the attacks

Martin Luther, or the fear of God

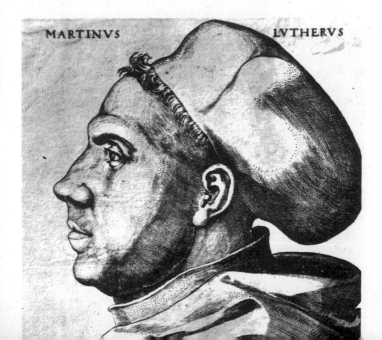

MARTINVS   LVTHERVS

which he found in them against the reformers Jean Oecolampadius (1482–1531) and Ulrich Zwingli (1484–1531) seemed to prove to him that he still adhered to the doctrine of Rome, and he felt it was not worth while going further into the matter. 'When I was beginning,' he wrote, 'to emerge a little from the darkness of Papacy, and had received a slight taste of sound doctrine, I read in Luther that Oecolampadius and Zwingli left nothing in the sacraments but bare and empty figures without reality. I confess I took such a dislike for their writings that I long refrained from reading them.'[7]

While he was trying to select a subject for the studies which would enable him to give proof of his mastery as a scholar, he had unexpectedly to rush back to Noyon. There he was present at the death-bed of his father (26 May, 1531), who had been excommunicated after quarrelling with the Chapter of the Cathedral over an obscure affair of succession. His family was put in a humiliating position, and only after his heirs had promised to meet his debts, was permission received for his remains to be laid in consecrated ground. But though these painful proceedings made Calvin feel somewhat bitter towards the canons of his native town, they did not precipitate his conversion.

With the provision made for him by his benefices and his share in the estate, he settled down in Paris, and in spite of his weariness of heart, he experienced some undisturbed months. He lodged at the College of Fortet opposite Montaigu. He now gave up all thought of trying further to develop his virtuosity as a dialectician, and he completed the education he had received from Cordier, Wolmar and indeed Alciati too. His new teachers, the Royal Lecturers of the College of France recently appointed by Francis I, were the hellenist Pierre Danès (1497–1579), Francois Vatable (*d.* 1547) the Hebrew scholar, and Guillaume Budé. Here were men, outstanding yet unassuming, who in their teaching refrained from expressing their own particular ideas but devoted themselves to the progress of the arts and to the elucidation of the precious ancient texts so recently restored in their original purity. Calvin had a burning desire to gain their esteem, and perhaps to be treated by them as an equal. He

Commentary on the De Clementia, *published in* 1532 *by a publisher in the Rue Jacob*

L. ANNEI SE=
NECAE, ROMANI SENATO=
RIS, AC PHILOSOPHI CLARISSI=
mi, libri duo de clementia, ad Ne=
ronem Cæsarem:

Ioannis Caluini Nouiodunæi cõmentarijs illuſtrati.

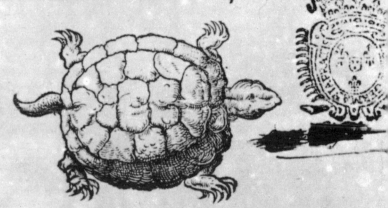

TECVM HABITA.

Ex Libris Sancti Germani à pratis.

Parisijs apud Ludouicum Cyaneum ſub
duobus Gallis in via Iacobæa.
1532

a a i

resolved that he too would become a careful and fluent commentator. Having chosen the *De Clementia* of Seneca he put all his skill and enthusiasm to work night and day. He embellished it with glosses and published the fruit of his labours in April 1532.

SENECA

This meditation on the *De Clementia* must not be under-estimated. It is no mere college essay written as a gratuitous display of cleverness. It gave Calvin the opportunity of proving himself a master and of realizing how far his gifts could carry him. Subtle philological comments are suggested to him by each maxim and aphorism of Seneca, and to these are added citations borrowed from the Bible, from the Church Fathers and from the great writers of classical antiquity. He analyses the rhetorical figures which this greatest Latin Stoic was too fond of using. Thus he perfected a method of interpretation that brought out the relevance of the text, being thorough and yet never losing the human touch. He now needed only to apply this same method to the difficult parts of Holy Scripture to become the founder of modern and positive biblical exegesis.

I must add that the *De Clementia* shows us clearly what is distinctive and outstanding in the character of Calvin. In spite of his youth he writes here with peremptory self-assurance. He flatters himself with having cleared up difficulties of which the great Erasmus himself was not even aware. He scarcely admits the possibility that anyone could question the correctness of his views. Without any hesitation whatever, he lays himself open to the charge of being conceited. Besides all this he betrays a certain aristocratic distaste for the people as a political force. He judges them to be seditious and stupid, and declares his preference for rule by a king where royal power is moderated by the strict and careful observance of political morality. Even in making this qualification, Calvin remembered the principles laid down by Pierre de l'Estoile and affirmed that the sovereign, being the living embodiment of the law, does not require to submit to restraint by civil laws. He finally defines a tyrant as a reprobate, who, in abandoning all care for the common good, seizes his power by brutal and lawless means with no greater aim than the vile satisfaction of his own personal lusts.

CONVERSION

By 1533 Calvin had in hand the tools with which his destiny was to be shaped. He was equally proficient as a dialectician, jurist or theologian. Anxious as he was to pursue his religious pilgrimage alone and to show respect for the manifold tokens of the working of the Holy Spirit within himself, he never considered that he could completely divorce himself from the times in which he lived. Thankfully he reminded himself of the inspiring things he had learned directly or indirectly from some of the French minds of the pre-Reformation days. His heart warmed that these men had been what they were. At that date he had not yet charged them with lack of courage. He felt for

Le nouueau Te-
ſtament/auquel eſt demonſtré noſtre
Salut eſtre faict par Jeſu Chriſt: annonce de Dieu
a noz Peres anciens des le commencemēt du mon-
de: et en pluſieurs lieup preduct par les Prophetes: Auec la declaration des œuures
par leſquelles lhome peuſt eſtre
congneu: et en foy et des
autres eſprouue fi-
dele ou infi-
dele.

❧ En la page ſupuante commence la Table des
parties de la ſaincte eſcripture recitees
en Legliſe au long de lannee.

them the reverence of a pupil for devoted teachers. There was Lefèvre d'Étaples (1455–1536), searching out the true meaning of the Scriptures, showing where they are figurative, explaining the allegories, translating the principal passages to give preachers great and vital themes for their minds to work on. Calvin admired this man, who, though he had refrained from expressing the opinion that good works are useless for salvation and exposing the scandal of monastic vows, had nevertheless weakened the authority of the Church by asserting that the ineffable secrets revealed to the personally enlightened were of more value than the speculations of the Fathers, and had disapproved of purely ritualistic devotions and of bold appeals to the saints' intercessions. There was Anémond du Coct (d. 1525), whom he had admired for his courage in trying to make the writings of the German reformers known in French territories. There were the adept dissenters from the community at Meaux, Pierre Caroli, and Martial Mazurier, who, uncompromising yet without fanaticism, even reproached their own master Lefèvre d'Étaples for being too indulgent, and were not afraid to give their people a healthy shock by preaching sermons commenting on evangelical doctrines suspected as heretical. There was Marguerite d'Angoulême (1492–1549) who, in her *Mirror of the Sinful Soul* was not afraid to take the most dangerous maxims of Lutheran mysticism and adorn them with the overflowing embellishments of her poetry. Calvin admired her most highly for her virtuous boldness. He wished too at times that he could do something to back up the venture of Gérard Roussel (?1480–1550), who was trying to persuade the Catholics of the great advantage that could come through a reformation without schism. He deplored the horrible death of Louis de Berquin (1490–1529), who bore faithful witness at the stake to the religious beliefs in which he found comfort.

Thanks to the information that came to him through his intercourse with humanists in various countries, he had at his disposal a volume of reliable political information, and he did not allow himself to be intimidated by fear of an immediate and

fevre d'Etaples searching out the true meaning of the Scriptures (Translation of the New Testament, 1530)

cruel repression. He was not unaware that the Peace of Cambrai (1529) which provisionally suspended hostilities between Francis I and Charles V, seemed to give the assurance that for several decades tolerance would prevail in matters of religion. He thought he had good reason to believe that the Emperor looked on himself as the external bishop, the temporal head of Christendom, and that, drawing his inspiration from the irenical advice of Erasmus, he wished to suppress error and bring about a reconciliation between believing men of good will.

Meantime the federated Lutheran princes (League of Schmal-kald, 1531) with Luther's agreement were setting up an evangelical Germany against the imperial and catholic Germany. By the treaty of Nuremberg (1532) the landgrave of Hesse obtained the suspension of measures taken against dissenters by the central authority. Francis I offered his good offices to the trans-Rhenish principalities in order to re-establish religious peace among themselves. This move had the result of increasing the influence of the League of Schmalkald and of bringing fresh assurance to all the French who were anxiously following all the various events in the outcome of its enterprises.

In these circumstances, apparently favourable to the Reformed cause, one of Calvin's friends, Nicolas Cop, Rector of Paris University, and son of Guillaume Cop (cf. p. 13), gave his inaugural address for the new term in the Church of the Mathurins on 1 November, 1533. This address gave deep offence. The theologians of the integrist school, who found themselves among his audience, were shocked at being forced to listen to such ill-chosen statements as these.

> 'Blessed are the poor in spirit' (Matt. 5). . . . And first of all, what we must find out most carefully is the aim of this Gospel, and how everything is related to it. It is easy to do so if we first of all define the Gospel and define the Law and then compare them with each other. Consequently the Gospel is the good news and the saving preaching of Christ proclaiming to us that He has been sent by God the Father to bring His help to all and to assure us of eternal life. The Law is contained within the commandments: it threatens us, it compels us, it contains no gracious promise. The Gospel makes no threats, does not bind anybody with precepts, teaches the sovereign goodwill of God towards us. Whoever consequently wants to give an un-tarnished and exact interpretation of the Gospel must not go beyond these definitions. Those who do not follow this way of understanding these things will never succeed in becoming conversant with the philosophy of Christ.[8]

Although Nicolas Cop's sermon was not, as has been believed for a long time, written by Calvin, the latter had at least followed

29

and looked over its composition and had provided his friend with the extracts he used from Erasmus and Luther. The whole text is marked by a rather suave gentleness, a moderation that lacks backbone, and a forbearance that savours of weakness. It reflects the attitude cultivated by the rather fastidious evangelicals who were gathered round Marguerite d'Angoulême and who dreamt of cleansing the Church and at the same time sparing it the torture of being torn apart in schism. We can conclude that at this date Calvin still hoped to further a reformation without violence, an achievement to be brought about by the pious men of letters of all nations and the new German theological doctors all working together.

But exactly six months later, on 4 May, 1534, he reappeared at Noyon, and resigned all his benefices, leaving them in the hands of the cathedral canons, as if he no longer wished to

receive financial help from the Church of Rome which he now looked on as a teacher of fallacies. What had happened to him?

His complicity with Nicolas Cop having been established, the threat of prosecution made him take refuge near Angoulême in the house of one of his friends who put a fine library of religious works at his disposal. He had conversations with the evangelical preachers who belonged to the Queen of Navarre's intimate circle. He came to the conclusion that it would be a serious sin for him to go on giving a formal public adherence to the teaching of Rome. He had been struck by an irresistible grace whose lightning stroke had reduced to ashes his strongest scruples. He received at the same time his call to be a doctor of the Church. Now a wanderer and an outlaw, although he tried as best he could to conceal himself and keep his movements secret, a large crowd of nameless disciples gathered round him and grew more and more—an ardent throng of thirsty souls.

Since it happened [he wrote] that I was so obstinately devoted to the superstitions of the Papacy that it was only with the utmost difficulty that I could be drawn out of such deep mire, God by a sudden conversion subdued my mind and made it teachable, for, considering my age, it was far more hardened than it should have been. Having then received some taste and knowledge of true godliness, I was immediately inflamed with so intense a desire to progress that although I did not altogether abandon other studies yet I had much less interest in pursuing them. And I was quite amazed that before a year had elapsed all those who had some desire for purer doctrine were continually coming to me to learn, although I myself as yet was only a beginner, newly enlisted. For my part, since I was by nature somewhat rustic and shy, I had always loved shade and retirement. I began to seek some hiding place in order to withdraw myself from people, but so far was I from finding my desire fulfilled that all my retreats became like public schools. In short, while it was always my ambition to live in seclusion without being known, God has so led me about by different turnings that He has never allowed me rest in any place whatsoever until, in spite of my natural inclination, He brought me out into the light, and made me play my part, as the saying goes.[9]

This sudden breaking in of divine grace certainly gave Calvin the assurance that he had the good will of Heaven on his side, and it relieved his melancholy. But he did not cease time and again to reproach himself in agonizing moods of repentance for having dallied and put off surrendering himself to the will of the Lord. He humbly confesses his sin in sentences such as these:

> When my mind was now prepared for serious attention, I began to realise, as if light has broken in upon me, in what a quagmire of errors I had wallowed and defiled myself and with what filth and shame I had covered myself. As for me then, as in duty bound, being exceedingly alarmed at the misery in which I had fallen and even more at the apprehension of the eternal death which threatened me, I esteemed that there was nothing more urgent than, after having condemned with tears and groans my past way of life, I should have recourse to Thy mercy. And now, O Lord, what is left to me, poor and wretched except to offer as my only defence to Thee my humble supplication that Thou wilt not reckon against me such fearful abandonment and estrangement from Thy Word, from which in Thy wondrous kindness, Thou hast at last delivered me?[10]

SECTARIES

Calvin felt he was a hunted man and that although Francis I pretended to be indulgent there was no place in France now where it would be possible for him to live in safety for any length of time. Hoping for more favourable days to come, he meanwhile forced himself to live a wandering life. But these toilsome journeyings did not in any way weaken the vigour of his intellectual life. His wish was that God might grant him the necessary leisure to put together a work in which he would 'institute' or establish article by article the true Christian doctrine, and he already had dreams of working this out. But at the same time he took deeply to heart the scandal that too many sectarian groups were propagating their false ideas throughout Europe. He found time during a brief stay at Orléans (autumn 1534) to refute the bizarre notions of certain fanatics who claimed 'that the souls die with the body, and that they rise again for the last judgment.' He does not spare them. He declares that they 'spring from the scum of the anabaptists.' He gives an arrogant justification for the violence of the polemical style which he intends to adopt every time he has to fight for the Lord's cause, and he does not hide his disgust for 'these individuals who have such a passion to embrace arrant nonsense, to snap like dogs and howl insults.' 'And if you as much as lay the tip of your finger on them,' he adds, 'they set about howling that you are shattering the unity of the Church and committing an outrage against love. Our reply to these people is . . . that no possible unity can exist if it is not found in Christ, and that there can be no love of which He is not the sole bond.'[11]

Thus, as early as the autumn of 1534 Calvin already had some idea of the important part that he would never cease to play in the Protestant Church. His task was to define for this Church her faith, and to secure her orthodoxy against the attacks of her many foolhardy or treacherous enemies.

'THE INSTITUTES'

But where was Calvin to find the quiet place where he would be allowed to produce this manual for the reformed Christian? After the affair of the placards (17 and 18 October, 1534), Francis I decided to override all the polite qualms of the chivalrous monarch within himself and to brandish the Sword of State against some sedition mongers who had been guilty of making an attempt against the royal majesty. In January 1535, Calvin arrived at Basle, the town of this Oecolampadius whose rashness he had detested, the city of Erasmus and the great printers. He set foot there at the very moment when, back in France, the fires of martyrdom were beginning to blaze. It was in the glare of those that he put pen to paper and drafted the first rough outlines of the book which was to become the doctrinal charter of Protestantism in Western Europe: *The Institutes of the Christian Religion*. He gives his own account of this with his usual sobriety and with a kind of furtive uneasiness which used to come over him when he resigned himself, in spite of his own personal inclination, to speak about himself:

And in fact, leaving my native country I took myself to Germany so that, hidden in some obscure corner, I might enjoy a peace that had been for long denied me. But lo! while I remained hidden at Basle and known only to a few, many faithful and holy persons were burned alive in France, and when the news of these spread abroad among foreign nations, they excited strong revulsion amongst many of the Germans who were roused to indignation against the authors of such tyranny.

In order to diminish the rumours, some miserable pamphlets, full of lies, were circulated, stating that nobody except Anabaptists and seditious persons were treated with such cruelty since, because of their ravings and fallacies, they upturned not only religion but also any political order.

As for my own position, I knew that all this deceit was the work of the tricksters of the Court whose purpose was not only to cover over the shame of such shedding of innocent blood, burying it under the false charges and calumnies which they brought against the holy martyrs after their death, but also to prepare the way for themselves in the future to go to all lengths in butchering poor saints without arousing the pity of anyone. Therefore I felt that for me to be silent would be cowardice and treachery and that I could have no excuse unless I opposed them to the utmost of my power.

These were the reasons that induced me to publish my *Institutes of the Christian Religion.* First, to reply to these wicked accusations that were being made and to clear the name of my brethren whose death was precious in the sight of the Lord. And next, since the same could very soon break out against many more poor souls, that foreign peoples might at least be touched with some compassion and care for them. Neither was it then when I published it, the large elaborate work it now is (1558), but it was only a little handbook containing a summary of the most important items; nor was it published with any other aim than that men might know what was the faith held by those I saw cruelly and evilly reviled by those impious and faithless flatterers.[12]

In that text Calvin shows clearly—and nobody would think of questioning his good faith—that it was not out of a vain wish to attract attention that he decided to hasten the publication of his theological views, but out of the burning zeal of his love. The proof of this can be found, when, to mark the occasion of the publication of his book, he wrote on 23 August, 1535, a respectful dedicatory epistle to King Francis I. He there affirms that his first

> purpose was to teach a few elementary principles in order to help those whose hearts might be touched, towards the knowledge of true piety.
>
> But [he adds] seeing that the fury of certain wicked men in your kingdom had grown to such a height as to leave no room for sound doctrine, it seemed to me to be expedient to make the same book serve both for the instruction of those whom first I had thought of teaching, and also as a confession of faith to you, that you may know what this teaching is that so inflames the furious rage of those who are disturbing your realm today by fire and by sword.
>
> For I am not ashamed to confess that what I have given here is simply a summary of the very doctrine, which, according to them, ought to be punished by imprisonment, confiscation, exile and flames, and which, they cry out, ought to be chased right off both earth and sea.
>
> Well do I know with what atrocious insinuations they have filled your ears and your heart to make our cause utterly hateful to you. But you must reflect in your clemency and forbearance that no innocence either in word or deed could remain anywhere if it were sufficient merely to accuse.

Without defecting from the respect he owed to his rightful king, he reminded him that when the Kingdom of God is established, whatever the circumstances, it will overthrow the temporal States whose foundations appear to be most firmly established.

> But our doctrine must stand sublime above all the glory of the world and invincible by all its power, for it is not ours but that of the living God and of His Christ, whom the Father has appointed King that He may rule from sea to sea, and from the rivers even to the ends of the earth and so rule as to smite

the whole earth and its strength of iron and brass, its splendour of gold and silver, with the mere rod of His mouth and break them in pieces like a potter's vessel, according to the predictions of the prophets concerning the magnificence of His Kingdom: That He will destroy the kingdoms that are as hard as iron and brass and as glittering as gold and silver.

In spite of his youth, feeling himself invested with sacred authority, Calvin did not hesitate to treat Francis I as a keen new convert, a catechumen full of good will. He certainly gave him praise for his discernment of mind, but he did not neglect to remind him of the imperious way in which St Paul tests the correctness of a doctrine.

You yourself, by your own prudence, will be able to judge by reading our confession how far this reproach is not only malicious calumny but also quite shameless impudence. Nevertheless it is right to say something here which may dispose or at least assist you to read and study it attentively. When St Paul desired that all prophecy ought to be conformed to the analogy of faith, he laid down the surest rule by which the interpretation of Scripture ought to be tested. But if our teaching is tested by this rule of faith, we have victory in our hands.

Then, taking the Sovereign indirectly into his confidence in a moving appeal, he launched out on a description of the illogical inward state of abnegation and yet confident faith in which the reformed Christian finds himself.

For what accords better or more aptly with faith than to acknowledge ourselves destitute of all virtue in order to be clothed by God? devoid of all goodness that we may be filled by Him? slaves of sin that we may be liberated by Him? blind that we may be enlightened by Him? lame that we may be cured by Him? feeble that we may be sustained by Him? to strip ourselves of all reason for glorying that He alone may shine forth glorious and we may be glorified in Him? . . . Again what is more in accord with faith than to assure ourselves that God is a propitious Father, when Christ is acknowledged as a Brother and Propitiator? than confidently to expect all gladness and prosperity from Him whose ineffable love towards us went to such lengths that He spared not His own Son, but delivered Him up for us all? than to rest in the sure hope of salvation and eternal life, whenever Christ in whom such treasures are hid, is thought of as having been given to us by the Father?[13]

The first Latin edition of *The Institutes* was published at Basle by Platter and Lasius in March 1536, and was an unprecedented success. In nine months the printer's stock was cleared of every available copy. It was a book of 516 pages. Since the format was small, it could be easily handled and easily hidden. It gave a thrill to many supporters of the Reformation to have at hand such a catechism for adults, or, what was even better, a summary of all the spiritual resources that were theirs to enable them to live soberly in this present world and to prepare themselves for eternal life.

Calvin soon resolved to expand this abridged version into a comprehensive one. He looked on it as a handy and convenient framework with room for fresh insertions. It was to be the depository for his observations, conclusions and discoveries as his growing authority as a polemist, preacher and statesman was confirmed. He made it, in an indirect way, the diary of his own Christian life. He remoulded and enlarged it. He put it through successive editions of which there are as many in Latin as in French. Five years before his death, feeling himself overwhelmed by his too frequent illnesses and sensing that his end was approaching, he regarded himself as being perhaps discharged from the exhausting life's work of teaching to which God had called him. He tried to achieve his aim of a definitive edition of *The Institutes*. He succeeded at the cost of exquisite suffering. The edition appeared first in Latin (1559), then in French. Its value lies in its preciseness, its thoroughness, its inner logic, and—I dare to suggest—in its objectivity. It bases Christian orthodoxy on so firm a foundation that no controversy has ever been able to shake it to the point of danger. It made Calvin, to use a happy expression of Bossuet's, the 'second patriarch of the Reformation'. Later we will examine some of its important themes (cf. pp. 84 ff.).

GENEVA

But Calvin was unable to avoid being involved in the strife that characterized the times in which he lived, and in spite of his need of quietness for study he was never able after 1536 to devote his whole mind to revising and improving *The Institutes*. In spite of the irritation he felt about this, he was forced to give first priority to the temporal affairs of the Reformed Church and to ensuring its defence against threatening dangers. He realized that as far as France was concerned, if those who were well disposed towards the Reformed cause merely contented themselves with fanning their evangelical sentiments into a warm heart-glow, but at the same time took care not to allow this to break out in public, then all his own efforts would be doomed to utter failure. Therefore on the one hand he appealed to the converts who were ashamed, taxing them with their hypocrisy and calling on them not to take any more part in the Roman rites, while on the other hand he tried to find influential patrons and sanctuaries for those who were exiled, the number of whom kept on increasing through his own influence.

Geneva. '*I had resolved to pass quickly by this place without staying more than one night in the town.*'

Though his weak constitution was a constant obstacle in his way, he did not hesitate to undertake hazardous missionary journeys. As he prepared his itineraries he had to take account of the wars that were being waged between the rulers of the various territories. After a short visit to Ferrara he returned to France during a temporary lull in the persecution of dissenters. His aim was to reach and settle in Strasbourg, then a brilliant centre for the exchange of new ideas. But the war which was raging in Champagne barred his passage. He then made his way to Geneva (July 1536) with the intention of going from there towards the districts of the Rhine.

Since [he wrote] the most direct road to Strasbourg, to which I then intended to retire, was blocked by the war, I had resolved to pass quickly by this place [Geneva] without stopping more than one night in the town. A little before this, Popery had been driven out of it by the labours of that excellent person, (Farel) whom I have named, and of Pierre Viret (1511–71). But things had not yet settled down into true order and the city was divided into vicious and dangerous factions. Then one man

Farel. 'That excellent person.'   *'Pierre Viret'*

[his friend Du Tillet] who now [1558] has basely apostatised and returned to the Papists, discovered me and made me known to others. Upon that, Farel—since he burned with an extraordinary zeal to advance the Gospel—immediately strained every nerve to detain me.[14]

Calvin, in his weak and distinct voice reminded him that as a frequenter of libraries he wished to pursue the solution of certain difficulties, the nature of which he had merely indicated in *The Institutes*. But he did not ward off the eager insistence of the man who faced him.

And, after having heard that I was given to private studies for which I wished to keep myself free, when he saw that he gained nothing by entreaties, he went the length of uttering an imprecation that it might please God to curse my retirement and the tranquillity for study which I sought, if in such an urgent situation of need, I withdrew and refused to give succour and help. At these words I was so staggered and appalled that I desisted from the journey I had undertaken. Nevertheless, conscious of my natural reserve and timidity, I did not want to bring myself under obligation to fulfil any particular office.[15]

However, in spite of all his natural aversion, circumstances forced him to throw aside his reserve. It is true that Guillaume Farel (1489–1565), truculent pastor that he was, had spent himself heart and soul. But Geneva was a place where the Catholic resistance was headed by men of intellect and vigour, and there was need for a leader who would organize the Church and put new life into it. It so worked out that Calvin was at first happy enough to acquire the teaching experience he had hitherto lacked and to let his influence be felt quietly in the humble role of lecturer in Holy Scriptures in the Church of Geneva. But as he discovered the abysmal ignorance of his hearers so he found himself to a gradually increasing extent delivering sermons and intervening in the legal disputes where his expertness in canon law enabled him to form wise judgments. Thus, to the fame of his theological teaching he added untiring service as preacher and ecclesiastical lawyer.

On 16 January, 1537, with the assistance of Farel, he submitted for the approval of the various councils of Geneva, articles on Church government. These reveal a combination of profound thinking and striking originality.

In his view, a Church should not be merely a body of clergy charged with the faithful proclamation of the Gospel and the right administration of the sacraments. It is, rather, a living and self-conscious community seeking in the midst of its inevitable imperfection to reflect prophetically something of the life of the Kingdom of God. Those who rule in it, in their concern for the growing sanctification of its members, will take care to gather them as often as possible round the Holy Table to attest the real presence of Christ, excluding at the same time those unworthy of such attestation. In this way the right of excommunication becomes, according to Calvin, one of the essential notes of all properly constituted Churches.

It is certain that a church [he wrote] cannot be called well ordered and governed, unless the Holy Supper of our Lord is celebrated often and frequented by the people, and this done with such good order that no-one dares to presume to present himself except in sanctity and with deep reverence.

For this reason, and in order to maintain the Church in its integrity, the discipline of excommunication is necessary by which those who do not wish to submit themselves wholeheartedly to the Word of God in complete obedience may be corrected.

Moreover, it is very expedient for the edification of the Church to sing, in the form of public prayers, some psalms through which prayer may be made to God, or that His praises should be sung so that the hearts of the people might be stirred, and thereby encouraged to express themselves in similar prayers and praises and thanksgivings to God arising from the same inward affection.

Thirdly, it is very proper and in a certain manner necessary if the people are to be kept in purity of doctrine, that children from an early age should be so taught that they can give an answer for their faith, that the evangelical teaching might not be allowed to decline, but that the form of it might be carefully

Strasbourg

preserved and handed on from person to person, and from father to son.[16]

STRASBOURG

Such a request so firmly made, could not fail to provoke jealousy on the part of the civil authority. 'I have lived . . . ,' Calvin reports, 'amongst continual bickerings. I have been on an evening mocked by being saluted before my door with forty or fifty shots of an arquebus. How, think you, must that have astonished a poor scholar timid as I am, and as I have always been, I confess?'[17]

In fact, Calvin and Farel did take up the struggle with the magistrates, who brought it to a finish by sending them into exile (23 April, 1538). Calvin now reverted to his first ambition. His experience as an apostle at Geneva had been a blow to him, a lesson in humility which he accepted with good grace. For the second time he arrived at Basle, resolved that he would have no

more to do with an active life, and that here he would find what he had never ceased to long for—the leisure to be one of the learned.

But already he had become so involved in the life of the Church through his writings and his journeys of mission that he could no longer avoid becoming what he was; a man with a passion for souls and a born leader. He did not, however, neglect the opportunity of again taking up his work as a scholar, and he expressed his joy at being 'able with a good conscience to settle his debt to his vocation'. But he rejoiced too soon, for he had scarcely begun 'to live in tranquillity without taking on any public responsibility', than another Farel, Martin Bucer (1491–1551), the gifted minister of Strasbourg, jolted him out of his torpor. Bucer reminded him of Jonah, and warned him that no one can with impunity disobey God's call. There was a flock of some fifteen hundred of his compatriots exiled because of their faith, and in need of a shepherd. How could he despise this call when he himself had harassed the most timid of his French partisans with pressure to break openly from Rome, and when he himself had dreamed of making Geneva into the place of refuge for his persecuted fellow-countrymen? In order that these people might be kept faithful to their own heritage and tradition in spite of being immersed in the atmosphere of Germanic piety in Strasbourg, Calvin united them one to another by the powerful bond of a common French liturgy. He taught them to sing eight psalms of Clement Marot. He translated for their use five other psalms, the *Nunc Dimittis* and the Decalogue.

The powerful bond of a common French liturgy

Psalme CXXXVII.

Stans assis aux rives aqua ti
ques De Babi lon Pleuriõsmelan cho li
ques, Nous sou uenans du pays de Sion.
Et au millieu de l'ha bi ta ti on Où de
regretz tant de pleurs espãdismes: Aux saulles

A conventicle in the Cevennes (18th Century)

THE REAL PRESENCE

Calvin did not wish the controversy which was being waged amongst the Reformation theologians on the subject of the Eucharist to become a stumbling-block to his people or cause falling off. For their sakes, therefore, he clarified his doctrine of the Lord's Supper. Recalling, no doubt, certain of the theses of Duns Scotus (cf. p. 12), he affirmed emphatically the real presence of the body of Christ in this sacrament, but he distinguished carefully the two utterly different ideas of reality and materiality—a distinction which Bossuet, in spite of all the finesse of his genius, never quite succeeded in understanding.

Now if it be asked whether the bread is the Body of Christ and the wine His Blood, we reply that the bread and the wine are visible signs which represent to us the Body and Blood, but that the name and title of Body and Blood is attributed to them because they are as it were instruments by which the Lord Jesus distributes them to us.

This form and manner of speaking is very appropriate. For as the communion which we have with the Body of Christ is a thing incomprehensible, not only to the eye, but to our natural

A spiritual mystery
(Drawing by Rembrandt, after da Vinci, 1635)

sense, it is there visibly demonstrated to us. Of this we have a very apt example in an analogous case: our Lord, wishing to give a visible appearance to His Spirit at the baptism of Christ, presented Him under the figure of a dove. St. John the Baptist, narrating this fact, says that he saw the Holy Spirit descending. If we look more closely we will find that he saw nothing but the dove, in view of the fact that the Holy Spirit is in His essence invisible. Still, knowing that this vision was not an empty phantom, but a sure sign of the presence of the Holy Spirit, he does not hesitate to say that he saw Him, because it was represented to him according to his capacity.

Thus it is with the communion which we have in the body and blood of the Lord Jesus. It is a spiritual mystery which can neither be seen by the eye nor comprehended by the human understanding. It is therefore figured to us by visible signs, according as our weakness requires, in such manner, nevertheless, that it is not

a mere figure but is conjoined with the reality and substance. It is with good reason, then, that the bread is called the Body since it not only represents, but also presents it, to us.[18]

HOMESICKNESS FOR GENEVA

Calvin should have had his mind in some way taken off his recent sad experiences by the demanding work he undertook at Strasbourg. 'Although,' he assures us, 'I always continued to be like myself, that is, not wanting to appear before or to wait upon the great assemblies, yet I was carried, I do not know how, as if by force to the Imperial assemblies [Hagenau, Worms, Ratisbon] where, whether I willed it or not, I happened to find myself in the company of many people.'[19]

But though he was achieving in Europe a fame that was beginning to gratify him, neither this nor the active part he took in these religious colloquies could fill the unique place in his mind and heart that he had for Geneva. He dreamed about her with sadness as the place to which the Lord had given him a call, where, whatever he had thought at the start, he was still urgently needed. He affirmed that 'although for the present', he might be 'relieved of the charge of the Church of Geneva, that, nevertheless, ought not to prevent' him 'from holding out towards it a fatherly love and benevolence'. He goes the length of saying that he cannot 'draw away' his spirit from the place, 'nor love and hold it less dear than', his 'own soul'.[20]

SADOLET

Thus, when one of the most honourable prelates of the sixteenth century, Cardinal Jacques Sadolet (1477–1547), Bishop of Carpentras, sent to the Genevese a fatherly admonition to exhort them to come back to the fold of the Roman Church, Calvin lost no time in taking up his pen to defend the validity and propriety of his ministry on the shores of Lake Leman, and to refute certain charges which the ill-informed Sadolet in his anger had rashly made against him.

As for me, if I had been concerned to further my own interest, I would never have left your party. As for your honours, which I have never desired nor could I ever put my heart into seeking, I will not boast that I had the ability to attain to them, although I have seen several of my own age who have crept up to some eminence, some of whom I might have equalled, and others outstripped. It will suffice if I say simply that it would have been allowable for me in your midst to attain what I had desired above everything else, to be able to devote myself to study in something of an honourable and free condition.[21]

Then, making use of an illustration from warfare he pictures himself before God as an ordinary trooper in the midst of a panic-stricken company of soldiers. Even though it may not be his responsibility, for he does not have the rank of standard-bearer, such a man might find himself compelled, however, to lift up some sign round which to rally his companions.

Perchance he must not be reckoned a traitor who, seeing the soldiers routed and scattered, wandering here and there and deserting their ranks, lifts up their leader's standard and recalls

them back into order. For all Thine, Lord, were so scattered that not only were they not able to hear the command, but also it seemed that they had forgotten their Captain, the battle, and the oath which they had vowed. And I, to draw them back from such an error, have not raised a foreign standard, but that noble banner of Thine whom we must follow if we would be counted among the number of Thy people.[22]

GENEVA

After his recall in 1541 to Geneva, which greeted him at first with a triumphant welcome, Calvin settled down there and scarcely left it till the day of his death. In spite of the loving attentions with which Idelette de Bure, his newly-wed bride, surrounded him it was not without some feelings of agonizing sorrow that he returned 'towards the flock from which' he had been, 'as it were, torn away'. 'Which I did', he declares, 'with grief, tears, great anxiety and distress.'[23]

When we think of the various kinds of ordeal for which Providence was preparing him, this foreboding which so overcame him appears in the light of a prophecy of things to come.

Twenty-three years later, when he was breathing almost his last sigh, he recalled again with a resigned bitterness the insults which men never ceased to hurl at him.

I was recalled [he relates] but I had no less trouble than before when I wished to do my duty. They set the dogs at my heels crying: Here! here! And these snapped at my gown and my legs. I went my way to the Council of the Two Hundred . . . and as I entered people said to me, 'Withdraw, Sir, we have nothing to say to you!' I said to them, 'I will do no such thing. Go to, wicked men, kill me, and my blood will witness against you, and these very benches will require it!'

In spite of so many disappointments and bitter hardships, he persisted in remaining captive to a 'nation so perverse and wicked', because he was persuaded that 'God will make use of this Church, and will uphold it.'[24] For the rest, he felt it was hardly worth while groaning over the troubles and disappoint-

ments which befell him without any break. He contented himself with murmuring at times under his breath, 'If I cared to speak about the various conflicts since that time, by which the Lord has put me through my training, and by what trials He has proved me, that would be a long story . . .'

Elsewhere Calvin always treats his silent readers with such respect as to avoid boring them with useless words. I will imitate his prudence, and will refrain from drawing up any useless and detailed account of his struggles. Let us be content with the knowledge that Calvin, this supposed dictator of Geneva, up to the very moment of his death, saw himself each day faced with the sad necessity of 'carrying on some fight or other either with people outside or people within'.[25] I must now complete my portrait of him by showing how, after having constituted the Church of Geneva on a sound basis, he defended its evangelical orthodoxy against every theological heresy without neglecting to give the most diligent guidance to the consciences of the leaders and martyrs of Western Protestantism with whom he held constant correspondence.

THE ORDINANCES

As early as 20 November, 1541, he persuaded the Genevan republic to adopt a body of Church regulations—the *Ordonnances*. The preamble to this document clearly defines the general tenor of its teaching. The important matter is that each of the faithful must seriously consider his responsibility in his calling and should be able to pursue it without earthly hindrance and in the strict observance of the precepts of the divine law.

In the name of Almighty God, we, the Syndics, the Little and Great Councils, with our people, assembled by the sound of the trumpet and the great bell, after our ancient customs, having considered that it is a thing worthy to be recommended above everything else that the doctrine of the Holy Gospel of our Lord should be well maintained in its purity and the Christian Church kept in proper order, that the youth in future should be faithfully instructed, the hospital kept in good condition for the support of the poor, which things cannot take

54

place unless there is some rule and way of life by which each in his rank understands the duty of his office.

For this reason it has seemed well advised to us that the spiritual government such as our Lord showed and instituted by His Word, should be set out in a suitable form so that it can take place and be observed in our midst.[26]

ASCETICISM

If the text of this detailed book of rules is to be taken at its face value, the members of the Church of Geneva, where the political and social forms of all future Calvinistic societies were being tested and worked out in experience, pledged themselves, without doing violence to the gifts bestowed on them by the Holy Spirit, to a life of mortification and rigid discipline. Transforming their town into a kind of huge convent for laity, they

would pay careful attention to their dress and yet avoid display; deny themselves the excesses of gluttony; shun participation either in private or public balls; see to it that no one in their midst ever committed an outrage against decency; control their language; utter neither oath nor blasphemous word; allow no empty talk, obscene jest or frivolous song to cross the threshold to their lips; resort neither to bone-setters nor sorcerers nor female fortune tellers; purge the shelves of their public libraries, throwing out the dubious and carnal products of worldly poets and every book tainted either by Roman superstition or heresy. They were to attend frequent religious services in order to cultivate the inward habit of secret prayer at the same time as they went about their professional and domestic duties. With all their might they were to seek to keep their spirits free from bondage to the flesh, to keep their hearts aglow with ardent desire for the second coming of Christ in glory, not to bring into the presence of the Lord anything but prayers that were fitting and offerings that honoured Him. Finally they would look with suspicion on the kind of prayer that is spoken with a copious flow of words, which accustoms the soul to garrulity or to laziness or lays it open to the dangerous glamour of basking in its own inner light, and they would give their preference to the private exercises in devotion prescribed for them by their pastors.

This life of constant voluntary watchfulness, far from being a wearisome burden to them, would enable them to cast off their dark opinions, their sullen lusts, and their disturbing thoughts and preoccupations.

Indeed, on rising in the morning they were to say:

Whatever I am engaged in, may my chief end and purpose be to walk in Thy fear, to serve and honour Thee, looking for my well-being and prosperity from Thy blessing alone, so that I may attempt nothing displeasing to Thee. Moreover, while I labour thus for my body and for this present life, may I always lift my eyes higher, even to this: to the heavenly life which Thou hast promised to Thy children.[27]

But in the evening, far from dreading anything that prowls in the darkness, they were to bless the night, the bestower of all the blessings of restfulness.

Lord God, who hast created the night for man to rest, as Thou hast ordained the day in which he must work, may it please Thee to grant me grace so to rest this night in body that my soul may be awake always to Thee, and that my heart may be lifted in Thy love and that I may so resign all my earthly cares that I may find the comfort I need in my weakness. May I never forget Thee, but may the remembrance of Thy goodness and grace remain always engraven on my memory, that in this way my conscience may enjoy spiritual rest as my body takes rest. Moreover, may I not sleep to excess, indulging too much to the comfort of my flesh, but only so much as the weakness of my nature requires in order to dispose me for Thy service. Be pleased to keep me unpolluted as much in body as in mind, and keep me safe from all dangers, that my sleep itself may be to the glory of Thy Name. But since the day has not passed away without my having offended Thee in many ways, since I am a poor sinner, as all is now hidden by the darkness which Thou dost send over earth, be pleased also to bury all my faults by Thy mercy, so that by them I might not be confounded before Thy face. Hear me, my God, my Father, my Saviour, through our Lord Jesus. Amen.[28]

THE ENLIGHTENED

Calvin tried to prevent the faithful, whose consciences were under his direction, from stirring up sectarian strife and from toying with queer religious opinions. Anyone who indulged in dogmatic speculations opposed to the established doctrine was first of all privately warned, and if he then refused to come to repentance, Calvin's rule was that the exhortation to him should continue 'until more severe treatment be deemed necessary'. If he obstinately persisted, the reformer's advice was 'that he should be forbidden Holy Communion and denounced to the magistrate'.[29]

Such severity seems excessive to the lukewarm secular complacency of our age, but the reason for it is obvious. Those men of the sixteenth century were of heroic temperament. They were infatuated by their experience of a power to which they felt there could be no limit, and they were naturally inclined to eccentricity and intrigue. They formed themselves into close cells in which they could indulge at ease in their prophesying. The whole of Europe around Calvin was polluted by fraternities, some spreading 'enlightenment' and some scepticism. He lived in fear lest this influence should divert his gathered flocks from their wholesome paths of duty. When he compared the excesses of these enthusiasts with the more moderate errors which he laid at the door of the Roman Church he was inclined to show towards the latter an unwonted indulgence.

> The Pope [he wrote] does not take away the hope of eternal life. He tells men to fear God. He makes some distinction between good and evil. He acknowledges our Lord Jesus Christ to be true God and true man. But the sole aim of those people is to confound heaven and earth together, to reduce all religion to nothing, to get rid of all idea of human understanding, to deaden consciences, and to leave no difference between men and beasts.[30]

Calvin realized that when we are fighting, if we can understand how the enemy's mind works and what are his plans, the battle is more than half won. He tried, therefore, through a praiseworthy effort in polemical sympathy, to understand their way of conducting propaganda, and to analyse the style of their discourse. In this way, he compiled an account of religious psychology that would be difficult to nullify.

According to him the sectaries, who called themselves Christian, exercised a peculiar fascination over gullible and weak-minded people. They could produce a counterfeit of what was spiritual. Since their teaching was so exalted and refined that it could not be expressed by using common speech, they employed a language the key to which was known only to themselves. They coined slang mystical phrases, 'a jargon like that of the beggars

Wolves and robbers must be chased away

of the lodging-houses, intelligent neither to you nor to them. . . .
Besides the fact that they speak of nothing but the realm of
spirit, they have a language so strange that those who hear them
are immediately struck with astonishment, and they put this on
with the deliberate purpose of carrying their audience away with
admiration, and of dazzling their eyes with such vanities.'[31]

They carried out this act of seduction by means of bizarre
exegeses of the sacred writings. 'Since they want to make it
appear that they do not reject the Scripture, they have turned
the whole thing into allegories, and they wander all over the place
seeking out-of-the-way meanings, making out that a man is
really a horse, and that a cloud is really the horns of a lantern.'

Those who lent their ears to such stories were soon convinced
that 'they ought to lift them right up to heaven with the angels'
and the refulgence of hitherto unheard-of revelations so dazzled
their eyes 'that they can no longer distinguish between black and
white.'

Le baston pour chasser les Loups

Moreover, the sectaries were not so foolish as to initiate their disciples through one such experience into the full meaning of their secret tenets. Using any number of abstruse words, 'they conceal the meaning of these, and never reveal the underlying mysteries of abomination except to those who were already under oath. While they hold a man still in the state of a novice they keep him gaping, paralysed and open-mouthed without a glimmer of intelligence. Thus by craft they hide themselves under these evasive practices like robbers in their dens.'[32]

What kind of people became so misled as to apply for admission into the inner coterie of the sectaries?

Some were addicted to a 'stupid curiosity . . . and, not satisfied with the simplicity of the Scripture', indulged in flights of frivolous speculation, 'either to satisfy their frenzy of desire, or

to show that they are both subtle and highly intelligent'. 'The others' peevishly taking it into their heads that the Gospel is 'a bridle to keep them in restraint', desire 'to find some haunt' in which they might find it 'allowable to carry on their low-down practices'.[33]

With their refusal to contain themselves within the limits of an austere and meditative existence, such people by their presence could only disturb the delicately balanced harmony of a Christian republic. It was thus a matter of urgency to agitate against them with untiring vigour.

Calvin reminded the ministers, his colleagues, that it 'is not enough to provide for the flock of Jesus Christ and to feed them in good pasture if they do not also keep a look-out for the wolves and the robbers, in order to shout out against them and chase them away from the flock if they should want to come near.'[34]

As for himself, he allowed no consideration of any political advantage to prevent him from denouncing the evil influence of the sectaries. He well knew that they had powerful patrons, and it would give little 'pleasure to them all to expose them too'. But it was not his nature to be 'more cowardly than a dog who will not allow anyone to attack his master without at least barking'.[35]

When Marguerite d'Angoulême, the Queen of Navarre, gave shelter to the sectaries, he did not hesitate to point out to her all the deadly errors of those men, knowing at the same time that he risked incurring the disfavour of one who had sacrificed much to encourage the cause of the Reformation in France. Indeed, she let him know through a third party how displeased she was. Calvin justified himself in an exemplary letter. He first of all protests the respect he has for princes, and the esteem which he reserves for the noble enterprises of the sister of Francis I.

Those who know me [he writes] are well aware that I am neither so barbarous nor inhuman as to despise or to try to bring contempt upon the principalities, the worldly nobility, and whatever pertains to man's political life. Besides, I know the gifts with which our Lord has endowed you, and how He has engaged you in His service and used you for the advancement of His Kingdom, which gives me ample reason for honouring you and for holding your honour in esteem.[36]

Since Marguerite had forgotten herself so far as to declare that she would not wish to reckon among the officers of her court such a troublesome person as the reformer of Geneva, she drew from him a reply with a tone of haughty humility which adds a striking trait of character to the portrait of Calvin which I am trying to sketch.

As for your statement about not desiring such as myself for a servant, I confess that I am not the one to render you great services, for I have not the ability, and besides you have no need of them. But certainly the inclination is not wanting, and as long as I live I will always persevere in this purpose if it please God, and however you may disdain my service, that will not prevent me from willingly being at heart your humble servant.

For the rest, those who know me are well aware that I have never aspired to gain access to the courts of princes, inasmuch as I have never tried to attain worldly honour. Even had I made the attempt to do so, it might possibly have been in vain. But I render thanks to our Lord that I have never been tempted in this way for I have good reason to be content to serve so good a Master who has accepted me and kept me in His household, indeed, by appointing me to an office of such dignity and excellence, however contemptible it may seem to the world. I would be going beyond bounds in ingratitude if I did not prefer this state to all the riches and honours of the world.[37]

It was this position of evangelical responsibility which constrained Calvin inexorably to ferret out the sectaries even when they were lurking in illustrious hiding places.

I am quite persuaded that it is not your mind that in order to favour you I should betray the defence of the Gospel which God has committed to me. Wherefore I beseech you, Madam, not to be offended if, being constrained by the duty of my office under the penalty of incurring the offence of God, I have not spared your servants, without, however, addressing yourself.[38]

The various teachings of different sects of these enlightened ones had, in spite of all their explicit differences, one common characteristic; they eliminated the cross of Jesus Christ and reduced to nothing the efficacy of redemption in His Blood. Calvin saw in this disregard for the blessed sufferings of the Word, the root of all the poisonous teachings which were growing to the perdition of the faithful in the garden of Christianity. 'They do not hold that Jesus Christ has been true man, but rather, they make Him a phantom as far as His body is concerned.[39] . . . A fine beginning that—making out Jesus Christ to be a phantom from whom we learn nothing of any consequence!'[40]

THE SPIRITUAL LIBERTINES

Certain sectaries, the spiritual libertines, held 'that there is only one existent spirit, that of God, who lives in all creatures.'[41] Thus, making man divine they attributed to each of his actions a peerless excellence. Comparing themselves to Christ they held all human activity as worthy of reverence including all their own works and deeds and those of their neighbours. They abstained from passing condemnation on anything. It suited them to suspend indefinitely the exercise of their judgment. In so far as they believed themselves all to be little bits of God, with each individual retaining within himself the fullness of divinity, so in the same way they abolished all distinction between good and evil.

Either we would have to impute sin to God, or we must resolve that there is no such thing as sin in the world, since there is nothing of which God is not the author. In this way, you see, all distinction between good and evil is taken away. Then it follows that it is not lawful for us to disapprove of anything as evil since everything is the work of God. For example, has anyone practised lewdness? We must not reprimand him, for that would be blasphemy against God. Does a man covet his neighbour's wife? Let him enjoy her if he can, for he can rely on himself to do only the will of God, and precisely whatever he does will be a divine action.[42]

The magician of Catherine de Medici

THE MAGIS

The Magis made up the second group of sectaries in whose teaching Calvin saw a menace to its adherents. Amongst them he took especial objection to the astrologers whose wild prophecies were at that time everywhere in vogue. Calvin, indeed, like most of his contemporaries, believed that all things which fill the cosmos, inanimate or living, are united to each other by mysterious affinities. He admits, without even discussing it, that 'terrestial bodies and all the lower creation in general are subject to the order of heaven so that they derive certain qualities from it.' He frankly acknowledges that, 'as far as the constitution of men is concerned and, above all, the maladies which share the qualities of their bodies, they depend partly on the stars, or at least have some correspondence to them.'[43] He does not dispute the legitimacy, or indeed the usefulness, of astrological medicine, but he teaches us to draw a line confining the influence of the stars 'to what is mundane and pertains to the body and arises out of the elementary movement of nature, but excluding whatever God gives in His special providence to one and another without using ordinary means, and, above all, the reformation of His elect which He brings about by renewing them with His Spirit.'[44]

In controversy, he never tires of denouncing the imposture of all the fortune-tellers who, 'good at emptying the purses and filling the ears . . . profess to know from a man's birth what lies ahead of him.'[45]

To show the ineptitude of their utterances, he allows himself to be carried away in an outburst of sarcasm which disconcerts us with its unusual truculence. Among several examples he brings forward one which seems to him irrefutable.

History tells us [he writes] that in a score of battles there died in Spain as many as three hundred thousand. Without going any farther into the matter, who would not jump to the conclusion that those who were involved in death together were indeed separated in their birth in the sight of the stars. Thus where such a host of people are concerned, the Goat, the Ram and the Bull collide on their horns with such force that everything is upset. The Water-bearer throws his water around so prolifically that there is a flood. The Virgin loses her maidenhood. The Crab crawls along backwards. The Lion wags his tail behind him but it is not noticed. The Twins get so entangled that they become one. The Archer draws a treacherous bow. The Balance proves false. And the Fish hide so still below the water that not a ripple is to be seen.[46]

But Calvin directs his anger especially against those with pusillanimous minds, who were unable to take the least step without first inquiring whether the face of heaven was favourable to them. One of the princes of the Church might happen to interrupt his supper to climb on horseback because his household astrologer urged him to do so, or a member of the council might not dare to straddle his mule if the evil influence of some planet threatened what he intended to do, or a merchant might put off the delivery of an order because he was turned back by the hostile disposition of the stars. It would be impossible to have condemned 'these speculative madmen' too much, for they had only themselves to blame for being victims of the mathematicians with their fabricated horoscopes. They 'do not consider what God is calling them to do, take no account of their office, turn away from the path which God is showing them, and forget the duty which they owe to their neighbour'.[47]

These craven souls, without any thought of guarding themselves against the dangers they incurred, became involved in a 'horrible labyrinth with no way of escape'. Calvin describes the inevitable consequences. 'Since the time they have even for one moment given loose rein to this curiosity, many unstable spirits after amusing themselves in the divination of the stars, shove their noses further in still in order to divine in all kinds of elements.'[48] With complete lack of concern they commit acts of sacrilege that are their own deliberate invention. Painstakingly they go through illicit ceremonies in their search for 'that revelation of hidden things attained through enchantments, either by conjuring up spirits or some other such vanity'.[49] Thus they fall into the serious sin of 'unabashed witchcraft'.[50] After having tried, through pride, to constrain the angels to pull them out of their difficulty, they try to secure the services of familiar demons. 'But', Calvin remarks, 'who has sold or hired out to them the devils to be their valets? For they are the deadly enemies of the children of God, and far from seeking any kind of communication with them, men should shun and chase them off.'[51] And he concludes with a last word on the matter, in which he warns all who court the Magis and practise magic of the extreme danger that threatens those who call upon the help of Satan:

'Those, then, who wish to make use of him, will find out at last that they have become the playthings of their masters.'[52]

SOBRIETY

As a spiritual counsellor, Calvin could not rest content merely with uttering such a warning. To those who confided in him he taught a golden rule for all intellectual honesty. For their sakes he took pains to show the real meaning of one word, to the use of which he was always partial—the word sobriety, this 'sobriety which Saint Paul recommends to us', keeping in check the disorderly impulses of the spirit, and showing love towards the weak things in the world around us.

Being a realist in every sense of a term which today has been debased, here is how Calvin, in order to undermine the satanic prestige of the occult, expresses his respect for the humble and just precepts by which the Christian life is controlled.

Whoever, in the first place, will devote himself to fear God and will study to know what His will is, will strive above all to practise what Scripture teaches us, then, secondly, will apply his mind to whatever his calling is, or at least to things good and useful, and he will not have the leisure time to indulge in flights into the air in order to hover amongst the clouds without touching either heaven or earth.[53]

THE HUMANISTS

There was a third and last sect whose influence Calvin set himself to thwart—those slightly disdainful clever people to whom I would like to give the name of worldly-minded humanists. As long as they calculated that the Reformation could help them to some extent to popularize the emblems of their own peculiar mythology, they supported it, but they tried to undermine it when they became aware that it bound the faithful never to overstep the limits which the Creator had set to their nature. It was not easy for them, however, to forget the Word of God to the study of which they had formerly applied themselves with zeal. In order to make it serve their purely humanistic ends, as Calvin puts it, 'it is as if all of them, or nearly so, should convert this doctrine of salvation into some heathen philosophy or other, which is an act of pollution that God cannot tolerate, for as much as His Word is something too sacred to be thus abused.'[54] They pretend to find in it things that justify their loose conduct. 'They hope to use it to pander to their desire for women.'[55] They argue that the 'rule of good living' is a 'licence for every kind of evil'. So much do they convince themselves that amongst their brilliant company 'the majority of those who claim to have known the truth of the Gospel . . . instead of having been made better, have rather become worse because of it.'[56] That is because from the very start, suffering from the humanist obsession, like new Titans heaping Pelion on Ossa in order to dethrone God, 'they have by their overweening and diabolical conceit, profaned this holy and sacred pledge of eternal life.'[57]

Calvin expresses himself as shocked that they, the enemies of every established Christian community, should dare to laugh at 'the folly and triflings of the Papists', when 'they are not worthy ever to return to the Papacy.'[58] He calls them 'mockers' who 'make a laughing stock' of all Christian hope, and propaganda material out of the facetious product of their wit. Whilst the spiritual libertines and magis of all kinds use the language of mystery, those men operate with 'snappy witticisms'.[59] Calvin, who often denounces the crudeness of the manners of the noblemen of his times, draws a picture of these worldly minded humanists in the role of self-appointed jesters, quick to seize their opportunity in the free atmosphere of the banquets to hurl their amusing epigrams, 'without appearing to have any other purpose except that of helping their audience to pass the time'.[60] Yet meanwhile in this way they pass on to them their harmful teaching. Conforming themselves to themselves, finding in man himself the one who both measures and fashions everything and every thought, they are not afraid to affirm that it is he who, being naturally endowed to concoct fables, invents the religions of the world, fashioning the gods as it pleases him, exalting them, casting them down and transforming them in the world of his fantasy; all of which makes the eschatological affirmations of the Gospel absurd and illusory.

SERVETUS

All the errors he had ever had to fight in his controversy with the sectaries were incarnate, according to Calvin, in the wretched Michael Servetus (1509–53). To be fair in our judgment of the action that was brought against him by the magistracy of Geneva, with the wholehearted approval and eager collaboration of the Catholic authorities of Vienne in Dauphiné, we must make a truly critical approach to the situation and not allow our-

Servetus

selves to be prejudiced by feelings of revulsion. We must not
expect from the theologians of the sixteenth century, either
Roman or Protestant, any spirit of toleration. They would
indeed have regarded such a spirit as being of the devil. Moreover, at that time everyone in temporal authority and every prin-
cipality in Europe regarded blasphemers as plagues which

69

spread the most deadly of evils through society by their contagion, and were thus capable of bringing about the speedy ruination of an earthly state. There is no doubt that in carrying through the condemnation of Servetus, to the applause of all Christendom, Calvin felt he was doing a work for the salvation of Geneva, indeed for the salvation of the City of God, of which that elect town was in his estimation the pulsating heart.

What, then, constituted the unforgivable blasphemies of the sectary Servetus? Calvin's own testimony is that this man was 'always shifting his ground . . . carried away by a mad and extravagant ambition'.[61] In this he is like the 'Anabaptists [cf. p. 33], libertines and suchlike'. Servetus is accused of trying to bring back into vogue the chimerical fantasies that were originally invented by the Gnostics.

Those of us today who are accustomed to expatiations on the poetic ramblings of our Nervals and Rimbauds, devotees of the most suspect oriental theosophies, will find ourselves moved only by curious amusement when we think of the fantastic falsehoods invented by Servetus. They produced in Calvin, however, the reaction of one faced by a horror revolting to the last degree, which makes it all the more necessary for us to acquaint ourselves exactly with the nature of his religious feelings.

What revolted him, among other things, was the suggestion that, according to this physician from Spain, God had 'so made His deity the property of all created things that He is wood in what is wood, and stone in what is stone[62] . . . that Jesus Christ has been so conceived of the substance of God in the womb of the Virgin that His divine substance has been turned into flesh';[63] that the Holy Spirit is 'a mixture composed of the essence of God and created force[64] . . . that man has a divine seed planted within him, not only with respect to his soul but also with respect to his body.'[65]

Moreover, he could not tolerate that Servetus should have made himself the apostle of the divine good will towards all religious men whatever their beliefs, that he should claim that 'the Turks do not pray any less well because they do not know or consider that God has promised them anything', and that he should go to the length of adding that 'all those who by the direct inspiration of nature itself have lived a good life, be they Jews or Gentiles, have been justified and reputed righteous before God.'[66]

DAILY ROUTINE

After the tragic end of Servetus, Calvin felt that all the claims made by the sworn enemies of the Gospel had been reduced to nothing. He now gave himself exclusively to clarifying aspects of his teaching that were still obscure, to improving the text of *The Institutes*, to the administration of the Genevan Church, to organizing a peaceful Protestant party in France, and to strengthening the morale of the communities he had set up in the majority of the countries of Europe. It is now time to leave off following the consecutive steps in the development of his thought, and to try to paint a characteristic picture of his life from day to day. For this we can obtain our information from two of his great contemporaries who were eye-witnesses: Theodore Beza (1519-1605) and Nicolas Colladon (d. 1586).

In face of the numerous chronic illnesses which overtook him, Calvin's aim was not so much to seek a cure for them as to ensure that, by uniting against them all the resources of a will of iron, they did not prevent him from carrying out the exacting duties of his calling. He presented to the citizens of Geneva an edifying spectacle as they watched his constant struggle against illness in the 'idiotic body'[67] which he had inherited at birth and which he himself had further weakened through the ascetic discipline prescribed by the regents at Montaigu (cf. p. 11). The heads of the State sent to his bedside the best doctors with orders to spare themselves no effort. They presented him with little casks of excellent wine in order to cheer him up. But so many anxious expressions of their care brought him little relief. His circulation was out of order. He suffered from hemorrhoids complicated by ulcers. His toes were swollen with gout. Chronic rheumatism forced him to hobble about dragging his right leg. He became at times transfixed by piercing pains due to stones in the kidneys. He had difficulty in breathing. He spat blood. He was regularly shaken by spasms of fever. But he would not tolerate any interruption to the work of his ministry.

He was 'an ever-taut bow'[68]—such was the nickname given him by the reformer Wolfgang Musculus—and when he felt that his own strength was going to let him down he pleaded with his friends to lend him a helping hand, or he tried to hoist himself up on to a quiet horse, or even, with extreme reluctance, gave orders that he should be carried about in a little chair.[69]

On Sunday, 10 May, 1556, although his fingers were seized by a convulsive trembling, he climbed into the pulpit and began to deliver the sermon he had prepared. His limbs became weak and he was threatened with a fit of fainting. He clung on. He asked somebody to pass up a folding chair. He sat down. He went on speaking in a muffled voice. But since his body was being shaken by violent jerks he saw that there was nothing left for him but to give in. They carried him to his house. There he followed his usual custom and subjected himself to rigorous fasting. He remained for two days with neither food nor drink. But then the doctors became alarmed at the 'extraordinary dryness' which was tending to drain away his 'humours', and they ordered him to take at least 'a dish of soup'. He consented, 'but some hours later his migraine'—his usual affliction—seized him and gave him 'almost as much misery as the fever'.[70]

He hardly knew what sleep was. At five or six in the morning he arranged on his bed the books he was going to need, and started dictating again to his secretary, from where he had left off, a further part of one of his theological treatises, and all the while hot fomentations were being applied to his ailing parts. Visitors incessantly interrupted him, but his unequalled memory, and his presence of mind stood him always in good stead. As soon as his interviewers disappeared he took advantage of the lull and took up dictating again. 'In most cases he himself remembered the place where he had stopped and carried right on with the argument without looking at what had gone before.'[71]

Fearing that his weak stomach and his disordered liver might cease functioning, he not only abstained from certain 'ordinary meats' to which 'he had been very partial', but he compelled himself to become satisfied 'for several years, with one meal alone, and no more than this in twenty-four hours . . . never taking anything in between',[72] except that in the months preceding his death he took a sip of wine and swallowed an egg about midday.

Yet even all this bodily weakness did not keep him from preaching each week-day every second week, from delivering three theological lectures each week, from taking part in the sessions of the Consistory, from guiding the other ministers in the coherent interpretation of the Scriptures, from visiting the sick and comforting the dying.

He made deliberate efforts to correct his faults. He dressed in sombre clothing and declared that the chattels and standard of life of the poor would be enough to satisfy him, protesting that the Republic of Geneva was treating him too much like an exalted personage. Certainly 'his illnesses, some serious and some ordinary', had made him 'cross and difficult'. Moreover he had a natural inclination in himself to anger,[73] but he applied himself to transform this with 'vehemence', and this latter mood now and then seemed to bring about in him an access to the spirit of prophecy. Here is an instance of second-sight, reported by his friend, Nicolas Colladon.

In the month of December (1562) he had such a bad attack of gout for several days that on the day for the examination of ministers in preparation for the Christmas Communion, the eighteenth, he had to keep in bed, and they held their meeting in his bedroom. There had been during the night a strange wind which gradually increased in intensity all that day and the next, which was the Saturday, and abated only on the Sunday. Then Calvin, in the presence of several ministers, speaking of the vehemence of this wind said something which a few days later was found to be true. 'I do not know,' he said, 'what it means. But all that night, hearing this great noise, it seemed to me as if it was God who was beating a drum on high. I could not

73

lift the burden of this from my spirit; something of supreme importance is happening.' But about twelve days later the news came that on that very day, Saturday, the 19th, the battle of Dreux had been fought, in which it is certain that God was acting against the enemies of the Church—whatever one might say.[74]

FRIENDSHIP

Now that he was invested with the highest spiritual responsibility, Calvin was on constant watch that no appearance of arrogance or pride should turn any of his followers from him. It was to him a Christian virtue for a man to be able to enjoy himself. So, in order to dissipate the gloomy fogs of his morose humours he tried to indulge in some relaxation. When he wanted to recover his spirits he found time, when he possibly could, to arrange brief periods of recreation. He loved short walks. He who passionately hated the sharpers who devoted themselves desperately to their card games day and night, excelled in little games of skill and was quite expert at throwing the quoit. In the midst of this he would allow the faint traces of a smile to play about his pointed lips, would throw off the cares which were eating into him, would become 'all good nature', and 'gentleness', would 'bring himself down to the level of the little ones', and would 'bear with the infirmities and imperfections of others'.[75] Above all, in his familiar intercourse with others he would conduct himself with such tact and sympathy that 'no friend was ever left offended through anything he either did or said.'[76]

He had indeed a true instinct for friendship. He was early left a widower, and had no other close relation than his brother Antoine (d. 1573) the tragic affairs of whose married life annoyed and humiliated him. He therefore sought in the fellowship of one or two responsive souls the wholesome pleasure of a love free from reproach. His huge volume of correspondence frequently reveals him as a man of warm-hearted sympathy towards those whose friendship he cherished, and even the solemn terms in which he expressed himself do not always conceal a touch of pathos.

BOVRGVINVS
INVENTOR

He seemed not to be able to do without the company of those he loved, not so much because he wanted a friendly exchange of ideas with them as because their fellowship gave him the feeling of being at peace. When he was cut off from them, he meditated with the intensity of a mystic on the doctrine of the communion of saints in which, as far as this life could allow, he found the pitiless barriers of distance overcome. 'The desire sometime to enjoy your presence will still continue to linger with me, and I will not lose hope. But there is this comfort, that in our absence one from another, we will not leave off our converse one with another in spirit, being united in Him who brings together things that are far asunder.'[77]

Calvin, who tried his best to strengthen the courage of his friends and to train them to take their stand against a world which he goes the length of comparing with the devil, regretted at times that he had tried to ram his teaching into them with such force; he would now have liked to be able to pass on to them his love in order to help them as weak and unprotected children. 'Why are we not together, to spite Satan by meditating on the things which ought to cause us spiritual rejoicing and give us occasion for boasting more than ever when in the opinion of the world we are utterly beaten! But I am aware that you have no need of my fellowship in that, and besides I am saying this more to relieve my own feelings than to meet your need.'[78]

He knew that it is dangerous for anyone to shut up his hurt feelings within himself to hide them, for then they can act like poison on the soul. But he was so concerned for the moral well-being of his friends that he always hesitated to seek to relieve himself by selfishly overburdening them with his sad stories. 'I do not like to distress you, though I am compelled to unburden my heart with great reluctance, of a sorrow common to all the children of God.'[79]

Let me add that, as Calvin conceived his duty as a friend, it made no difference to him whether he was asked to do something big or something small. When one of his friends, a refugee, appealed to him to find him lodgings at Geneva, he threw himself into the task with an astonishing enthusiasm for domestic matters, taking care that the house which he chose should be large, well ventilated, with a pleasant appearance and above all that it should look out on to a comfortable little garden suitable for a recluse.

POLITICS

Calvin could not become involved as he was, by his ministry, in a turmoil of business on every side, without finding himself almost involuntarily at the head of an influential party. He found himself, moreover, constantly obliged to give both advice and warnings to members of an insolent and unmanageable nobility who thought they could use the differences about religion, which were troubling France, to secure their own worldly advancement.

It is true that in his political views he showed a constant preference for the aristocratic type of republic in which the magistrates, elected by a plural vote in council, were under the censorship of faithful pastors, and submitted to the injunctions of the divine law. But he forbade those who were subject to earthly monarchs to attempt to overthrow the regime, or to take any initiative, whatever the provocation, in rebelling against the royal authority. If men suffered injustice and persecution, he recommended them to implore help from heaven. In 1556 he adjured the Protestants of Anjou not to have recourse to arms and added:

> When I do not give my approval to such undertakings, I entreat you not to suppose that I am not concerned about you as I ought to be. The fact is that the friendship which I hold for you requires me to be frank with you. Just now I am even more greatly saddened and troubled because of the threats to which you are being subjected, and the further prospect, to which we cannot shut our eyes, of a persecution greater than anything you have experienced for a long time. You can be sure that many of your worthy brethren are concerned about you in the same way.

But we can only groan in prayer to God that it may please Him to save you by the hand of that good and faithful Shepherd to whose care He has committed you. . . . You must pray to Him for two things; that He will not allow you to be tempted beyond your power, and that meanwhile He will fortify you with such strength that, whatever happens to you, nothing will so dismay you as to cause you to falter. . . . Consider, too, that we have no excuse for refusing to suffer for Him who died and rose again in order that we might dedicate our lives as a sacrifice to Him. And although the world not only laughs at our simplicity, but also detests us, let us content ourselves that to bear witness to the truth of His Gospel is a service that pleases God more than any other thing.[80]

Towards the middle of 1559 when on inflamed and desperate Huguenot minority drew up the ill-conceived plans for the conspiracy of Amboise, they first of all sought reassurance from the reformer as to whether there was theological justification for what was in their minds. They asked him 'if it would not be lawful to resist the tyranny with which the children of God were then oppressed.' Calvin, overcoming his instinctive aversion, would concede only that 'if the princes of the blood royal demanded to be maintained in their rights for the common good, and if the courts of Parliament united in taking up their cause, it would be lawful for all loyal subjects to lend them armed assistance.' But he forbade them to foment any lawless uprising, and argued with them that it would be better for the French Protestants to perish 'every one of them a hundred times than to be the cause of exposing to such shame the name of Christianity and the Gospel.'

In order to persuade him not to be quite so rigid in his attitude they sent him no less a person than their ringleader, Godefroi du Barry de la Renaudie (d. 1560). Of him, Calvin declares, 'Having always known him as a man puffed up with vanity and self-conceit, I rebuffed him and remained distant so that he could never get from me the slightest sign of approval; indeed I rather strove to put him off this foolish course with many arguments which it would take too long to enumerate.'

A frightful legal massacre

La Renaudie's recruitment for the rebellion amongst the French refugees in the Swiss cantons grieved Calvin deeply. Shrugging his shoulders both in mockery and vexation he dubbed this 'a crusade of knights errant or of those of the round table who were truly bewitched.' When the whole lamentable affair ended up in a frightful legal massacre he was plunged into deep distress but he had to confess that the outcome had not taken him by surprise. 'For', he declared, 'I have constantly predicted the issue, protesting that I feared that at the end I would be known as too true a prophet.'[81]

This did not, however, prevent a persistent rumour in Court circles in France that he had instigated the riot. Charles IX wrote a letter to the Council of Geneva in which he blamed him indirectly for sending secret agents into France in order to inflame the bold. But Calvin in his reply stood by his colleagues, the Protestant missionary preachers who had been slandered in such an ill-informed manner, and, as if putting his own eloquence in their mouths, declared in their name:

> With regard to the charge of stirring up disturbances and seditions, they protest that they have never entertained any such purpose but on the contrary that they have taken trouble to do everything in their power to hinder and prevent any such outbreak from taking place, that they have never given their advice in favour of revolutionary change in, or overthrow of, the established order, but have exhorted and induced all who were willing to listen to them to remain in peaceable subjection to their prince.[82]

Calvin did his best to support the decision of the States General of Orléans where the Deputies of the Third Estate called

The slaughter at Vassy

for a Gallican council to be summoned, presided over by the King. Thanks to the assembly of the most level-headed members of the French nation, he had hopes that religious peace would be gradually achieved through peaceful consultation. But his attitude was changed by the massacre of Vassy (1562), an act of collective criminality for which the Guises and their confederates were responsible.

It cannot be denied that if this act of butchery had been perpetrated under the express orders of the King, Calvin, with his soul abhorring the atrocity of it, would have tolerated it as an act sanctioned by the inalienable right of royalty. But he did not believe that there was any call for such restraint when faced by such a hideous exhibition of tyranny by the family of Lorraine. He agreed to an appeal to his brothers in the faith to take up arms against these barbarians. He encouraged Andelot to raise an army. He exhorted the Church to unite in paying for its maintenance; 'for', he wrote, 'whatever the past may have been, God has reduced us to such an extremity that if you are not helped from this direction there can be no hope of anything, if we depend on men, but a tragic and horrible desolation.'[83]

Meantime he called upon the Protestant militia not to blacken their name by any act of excess, enjoining them not to slaughter prisoners. These were to be put into the hands of lawfully appointed magistrates after any action that might be deemed politic.

While he regretted that the edict of the pacification of Amboise (1563) negotiated by Condé (1530–69) assured liberty of worship only for individual gentlemen, he affirmed that he had decided never again to stir up his flock to revolt against royal authority. He went the length of deploring in a private letter that he had encouraged faithful Protestants to engage in the war against the Guises.

> I cannot conceal from you that everyone finds it hard that the Prince should have shown himself so accommodating and more so that he should have been in such a hurry for a settlement. It seems quite evident too that he has been more con-

John Calvin, aged fifty-three

cerned to provide for his own personal safety than to ensure
peace for the poor brethren. Be that as it may, this single fact
ought to make us silent when we know it is the will of God
again to exercise us. I would always counsel that arms should
be laid aside, and that we might rather perish than return
again to the chaos that we have witnessed.[84]

83

One month later Jean de Soubise consulted Calvin about the possibility of taking up the campaign afresh. He was taking advantage of the presence of Protestant battalions in Dauphiné. But his correspondent had no hesitation in giving him his answer.

> Besides even if they joined you, you would still need to be sure you had right on your side, for to attempt anything without our being called and led to do so, can never come to any good. . . . Meanwhile I do not say that you should quit the place (Lyons) at the very first summons, in order to throw yourself into the jaws of the wolf, but to act in direct opposition to the command of the King is something I do not see that God permits you to do. . . . I am aware of the disadvantages you allege, but for my sole answer I hold to what Abraham said, 'The Lord will provide.'[85]

The Lord was to see to it that John Calvin, His servant, was able to remain, without being too uneasy in his soul and conscience, a loyal subject to his most Christian Majesty.

THE INSTITUTES

When he wrote the words about submitting to Providence (April 1563), Calvin knew that he himself would soon pass through the gates of death. From the last weeks of 1558 he prepared himself for it. His concern was to make a definitive last edition of *The Institutes* (cf. pp. 33 ff) to which over a period of twenty-two years he had constantly added the fruits of his experience and his thinking. He associated himself with his brother, worthy Antoine, and some friends. He had periods of dangerous illness and concentrated all his will-power on counteracting their mental effects. He gives this striking testimony.

> When I was threatened by quartan ague with having to depart from this world, the more firmly the illness seized me, the less I spared myself so that I might finish the book which, surviving my death, might show how much I desire to satisfy those who already have profited from it and would desire to profit from it more fully.[86]

He revised and recast all the previous versions. Before August 1560, he had added the last touch both to the Latin text of his *magnum opus* and to the corresponding translation into French. It was only with much pain that he succeeded in absorbing the immense mass of material that he planned to expound. He managed to forget all personal feelings and forced himself to take up an objective attitude, avoiding incongruities. And so, behind all his exposition of the ordinary theological problems there is an unerring inward coherence of thought which gives an orderly arrangement to the whole.

This masterpiece of theological writing is still a source of vital inspiration for the theological thought of innumerable Christians of all countries and denominations, but in case my readers may now feel favourably disposed towards Calvin, I do not want to risk alienating them by trying to give here a summary of his doctrinal teaching—as has been done by so many who are either critics or over-zealous devotees of Calvin. I wish simply to select from his topics, and bring out some of the helpful thoughts that go to make up this evangelical treasure bequeathed to us by the great reformer of Western Europe.

THE FATHER

According to Calvin, we must avoid trying to capture God in a net finely meshed with philosophical arguments, for 'His essence is indeed incomprehensible so that His majesty is hidden far beyond all our human senses.'[87]

The knowledge of God which we should seek to attain is such knowledge as will lead us to fear Him, to revere Him, to love and to praise Him for the blessings which He unceasingly showers on men.

But the privilege of knowing God in this way can be experienced by us only as we allow ourselves to become learners in the school of Holy Scripture from which we can gain nothing that will be profitable to us unless first of all we have a living faith to help us to grasp it, since it is true also that 'the mysteries of God are understood only by those to whom it is given.'[88]

THE SON

Moreover, those who are accredited thus with faith do not find in the Bible a series of theoretical maxims or a mere collection of stories either scandalous or edifying, but on each page, as if in a crystal mirror, they see appearing the divine face of Christ in whom God reflects His own Self.

Thus they enter the fellowship of the elect, 'the saints of past days', who 'have never known God apart from beholding Him in His Son as in a mirror.'[89]

THE SPIRIT

If faith, however, is to have on them this effect, at once so secret and yet so evident, it is necessary that the Holy Spirit should enter the hidden depths of their heart with His illuminating witness, bringing them the assurance that the oracles preserved in Holy Scriptures are authentic and trustworthy. 'It is necessary that the same Spirit who spoke by the mouth of the prophets should enter our hearts with His witness in order to convince us that the prophets have faithfully delivered the message committed to them from above.'[90]

This witness of the Holy Spirit gives us a supernatural power to apprehend a God who would otherwise remain hidden from us through the innate perversity of our nature which prevents us from discerning what is witnessed to us in the magnificent theatre of the universe. Not only does Calvin deny that a man, left to his own inner light, can develop a natural theology of any significance whatever, but he also estimates as worthless the ramblings, sometimes seductive, of the heathen philosophers whose discernment 'was not such as to direct them to the truth, far less to enable them to attain it, but was nevertheless sufficient to make them without excuse for their impiety.'[91]

MAN'S WRETCHEDNESS

When he surveys our tragic original state Calvin abounds in eloquent and woeful lamentations which are moderated little by the implacable strictness of his logic.

Even if man had remained in his integrity his condition was too humble to enable him to penetrate to God without a mediator. How much less can he raise himself to such a height after being plunged through fatal ruin into death and hell, after being defiled by so many stains, indeed having become rotten in his corruption and overwhelmed with every curse.[92]

LOVE

Calvin, nevertheless, almost consoles himself with the thought that however detestable he may be, God recognizes him as one descended from Adam whom He has fashioned with such love and to whom He cannot deny His help. On this theme he rises to sublime heights.

> For God, who is perfect righteousness, cannot love the iniquity which He sees in us all. We have all, then, that within us which deserves the hatred of God. Hence with regard, first to our corrupt nature, and then to its consequence in our evil way of living, we are all offensive to God, guilty in His sight and born in damnation. But because God does not will to lose in us that which is His own, He yet finds something there which out of His kindnesss He can love. For although we may be sinners by our own fault, we remain always His creatures. Though we may have acquired death, He Himself nevertheless created us for life.[93]

Calvin gives expression to this mystery of the love of God in utterances that are deliberately equivocal, the profoundness of which will always kindle our admiration.

'As far as God Himself is concerned, His love precedes everything else in time and in order too. But from our own point of view the beginning of the love of God towards us is in the sacrifice of Christ.'[94] He adds: 'It is true then that God the Father forestalls and anticipates by His love our reconciliation in Christ.'[95]

He is impelled to give further expression to feelings that he finds hard to subdue.

> We have no full and sure union with God, except as far as Christ unites us to Him. And indeed if we want the assurance

that God loves us and is propitious towards us, we must fix our eyes and minds on Christ alone, since truly it is to Him alone that we owe it that our sins are not imputed to us which otherwise had provoked the wrath of God.[96]

All this leads up to a fine example of a didactic hymn in which the note of triumph is admirably sustained.

Therefore, to that union of the head and members, the indwelling of Christ in our hearts, the mystical union, we assign the supreme place. Christ, having become ours makes us share with Him in the gifts which are bestowed on Him in their fullness. Nor, then, do we simply look to Him as to one outside and distant from us, merely for an allocation of His righteousness, but since we are all clothed in Him and are inserted into His body, in short, since He has deigned to make us one with Himself, that is why we glory in having a fellowship of righteousness with Him.[97]

PREDESTINATION

The reader will find further on (pp. 115 et. seq.) a section of the important treatise on the Christian life which Calvin incorporates in *The Institutes*. This completes the few citations on which I have just given my comments. I would like now as a last touch to this portrait which I have sketched so inadequately, to give a brief account of the last days of the first pastor of the French Reformed Presbyterian Church. I cannot help remembering, however, that all his enemies, and some of his disciples too, are not afraid to reproach him for causing despair in men's souls by a harshness that comes from stressing theology instead of the Gospel. I must therefore briefly explain how it comes about that the believing man, even though he may not become entirely free from his perplexities, can at least find comfort if he can make the doctrine of the predestination of mortal men a part of his living confession of faith. But at the same time I would argue that the latter doctrine is not, as ill-disposed and ignorant people claim, the soul and substance of his theology.

Let me point out that what is supposed to be Calvin's system is not a closed and unified structure originating through the development of one sombre and revolutionary idea. Calvin, rather, allows all the winds of the Spirit to play freely on a great variety of biblical conceptions. As these branch out the one away from the other, under no circumstances can human rashness be allowed to clip them or lop them off. Calvin takes these one after the other, describes them, then explains them, leaving us the impression that they are indeed bound one to the other in a transcendent unity the key to which remains wrapped in mystery. But never does he risk trying to subordinate all these to some dominant and central doctrine—for instance to that of predestination. He is too much aware of the complex vitality of Christianity ever to fall into such a pernicious excess of sophisticated logic.

Predestination, then, is in his eyes only one—and not the principal one—of the ramifications of the biblical tree. In inquiring into it men 'penetrate into the inmost recesses of divine wisdom'.[98] Here if we are true Christians we will be restrained by his intellectual sobriety, and will make no attempt to probe the depths, but will rather offer without fear the adoration that is fitting. Nor will we allow any harmful anxiety over this matter to possess us, for each of us will confess 'how greatly ignorance of this principle diminishes the glory of God and detracts from true humility',[99] that is, when we do not ascribe the whole cause of our salvation to God alone. Thus we soon become aware 'how much this doctrine is not only useful but also produces most pleasant fruit'. In fact if we calmly reflect on the matter we perceive that divine election becomes gradually understandable 'because it illustrates for us by contrast the grace of God, in that He does not adopt everyone indifferently in the hope of salvation, but gives to some what He denies to others'[100], and we can at last experience in their fullness the imperishable joys of the faith, 'satisfying assurance of the eternal predestination of God, so that it would be a fearful sacrilege to inquire any higher, because whoever makes difficulties over giving assent to the simple witness of the Holy Spirit insults Him grossly'.[101]

Calvin himself as he lived through his last days was comforted both by his experience of the real presence of God through the eucharistic elements and by the witness of the Holy Spirit at the heart of his pastoral, moral and mental life. He was forced to give up his public teaching from Sunday, 6 February, 1564, onwards. His constant sufferings he rendered bearable by devoting himself to the exercise of unceasing prayer which he intermingled with simple exclamations from the Bible (he distrusted so much the vain imaginations of flesh and blood). 'Lord, how long? I keep silence, O Lord, for it is Thou who hast done it. I moan like the dove. Lord, thou dost crush me, but it is enough that it is Thy hand.'

He devoted the most careful attention to taking leave of his friends in a fitting way. On 25 April, 1564, he dictated a last will and testament praiseworthy for the sobriety with which it enters into details. He had already drawn up many confessions of faith to meet the need of the slandered Christians whose consciences he had directed. Now he turned his mind to drawing up an inventory of his beliefs and his hopes with the purpose of presenting it without any guile for the momentous judgment of his God. He dispelled from his brain the insidious mists of pride still lingering within it, and thought with wonder on the goodness of God towards him, trying to hide his emotion as he declared:

> He has had pity on me, His poor creature, to draw me out of the abyss of the idolatry in which I was immersed, so that He could bring me out into the light of His Gospel to make me participate in the doctrine of salvation, of which I was completely unworthy. . . . He has held me up amongst so many sins and failures for which I should have been rejected by Him a thousand times. . . . He has so far extended His mercy towards me as to make use of me and my labour to convey and proclaim the truth of His Gospel.[102]

But the memory of this high calling to which he again heard the decisive summons resounding, instead of bringing him comfort seemed to overwhelm him for a moment.

'*Take courage and fortify yourselves, for God will make use of this Churc*

Alas! the desire I have had and the zeal—if it must be so called—has been so cold and sluggish that I feel myself hopelessly in debt in everything and everywhere, and if it were not for His infinite goodness, all the affection I have shown would only be like smoke. Indeed even the favours that He has shown me would simply render me much the more guilty. My only refuge is in this: that being the Father of mercies, He will also be and show Himself the Father of such a miserable sinner.[103]

Knowing that he was surrounded by veneration he stipulated that he should be accorded only an ordinary funeral and an anonymous grave, so that his remains might never become a material cause for superstitious worship. Then he distributed his meagre possessions amongst the members of his family. And though he then considered his work finished, since his Master had deprived him of the strength he needed to continue it, he felt that it would not show disregard for the arrangements of Providence if he exhorted for the last time the Seigneurs responsible for the government of Geneva. He wanted to prevent his town-church from foundering in anarchy. They met with him again on 27 April, 1564, and he addressed them arranged round his bed, in a sequence of brief words of admonition, kindly and varied, revealing even in their tone that he had always encouraged friendly intercourse with them.

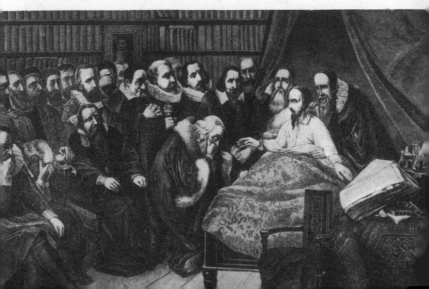

He asked them to excuse him, to forget his bouts of sudden anger, 'his natural disposition by far too vehement' which sometimes caused them trouble. In several neat sentences he deftly summed up their various characters. He reminded them that the well-being of their state demanded what was difficult to attain under its synodical constitution—that they should take pains to agree among themselves. To prevent the differences that threatened to divide them he taught them this threefold golden rule:

Let the old not bear envy towards the young for the grace they have received but let them be pleased about this and praise God for having bestowed it on them.

Let the young control themselves with modesty, with no desire to push themselves forward; for there is always a boastfulness in young folk who cannot bridle themselves, and push on in despising others.

Do not discourage one another, and do not hinder one another, and let no-one make himself odious, for when people become nettled they are led away.

And to avoid all troubles [he concluded], let everyone walk according to his rank, and set himself to work faithfully with what God has given him to maintain this Republic. [104]

On the following day, 28 April, he assembled the ministers, his colleagues, in his bedroom. To justify upsetting their arrangements, he gave them a startling account of the precarious state in which he found himself.

'When they take me to put me in bed my head fails and I immediately lose all consciousness. There is also this shortness of breath which oppresses me more and more.' [105]

Then he confided to them his fear of losing his power of speech, at the same time expressing confidence that God would not allow him to lose soundness of mind. Since it might be only for a short time that he had the use of his tongue he wanted to seize his present opportunity. He prophesied the lasting stability of the community which they were devoting themselves to build up.

'But take courage and fortify yourselves, for God will make

use of this Church and will maintain it and assures you that He will protect it.'[106]

Again he went over the method he had followed in his thinking, using words that were bound to remind his visitors how, although he broke away from the finesse of scholastic discussion, yet he could well have rivalled the most skilful sophists in quibbling over niceties; but in his own writing he had always tried to combine simplicity and sobriety.

As for my doctrine, I have taught faithfully, and God has given me grace to write—which I have done more faithfully in that it was in my power. I have not falsified a single passage of the Scripture, nor to my knowledge have I wrongly interpreted it. And when I might well have introduced subtle senses, had I studied subtlety, I put that all under my feet, and I always aimed at simplicity.[107]

Finally, in order that religious controversy might not degenerate into civil strife, he adjures his hearers to avoid venturesome speculations.

I pray you also to make no changes nor innovations. People often want novelties. Not that I desire for my own sake, out of ambition, that my way of things should remain, and that people should retain it without wishing for something better, but because all changes are dangerous and sometimes harmful.[108]

This whole scene of a sick man forgetting his own inward distress in order to proclaim the things of which he was so certain, was so charged with hidden emotion that those present, in spite of their long pastoral experience of the approach of death, were not able to avoid showing their feelings. An eye-witness notes: 'He took honourable leave of all the brethren who touched him on the hand, one after the other, all of them, bursting into tears.'[109]

In spite of his forebodings he lingered on till 27 May entering in spirit into all the public services of his church. He fell into a peaceful sleep and passed away quietly at eight o'clock in the evening. His body was sewn inside a shroud of coarse cloth without any ceremonies or speeches or hymns. The corpse was taken to the cemetery of Plainpalais. There followed an immense throng of people belonging to every class of society. Care was taken that no sign whatever should point to the unknown spot where lies, 'awaiting the day of blessed resurrection', the remains of Master John Calvin.

DIGRESSION

So far, I have tried to reproduce Calvin's own testimony to himself. It is with hesitation that I now add some observations of my own, in order to complete the picture. Yet I feel that the sympathetic reader must have already gained some deep religious impression from this life, and I would like to emphasize certain points.

No one has succeeded in giving a satisfactory explanation of what is almost a miracle, that Calvin in giving expression to his weighty thoughts uses what we might call a language of eternity which has survived the ravages of time, and under no circumstances loses its relevance. Whereas both the style and the arguments of Rabelais, his contemporary, have become to us equally obscure, yet with Calvin we are able to grasp even his most hidden meanings and we can interpret without difficulty the most fugitive of the allusions contained in his writings. This results from his style being so permeated with an instinctive geometric purity that he takes the greatest care to use only words from common speech and with obvious meanings, and to employ them in their simplest, most direct, clearest and purest sense. The remote jargon of the pedant is never allowed to disfigure or obscure what Calvin has to say, and he addresses himself not to a few insensitive dons proud of their knowledge, but to the congregation of those who are predestined to believe. His aim in clearing away the main difficulties of Scripture and in presenting his orderly argument is that in the minds and hearts of such elect the Holy Spirit should be given access for His intimate work.

It follows that the lessons to be learned from the writings of this great man prove themselves applicable to each age. Today when even the highest of our religious conceptions tend to become degraded through being parodied in a multitude of low and coarse ways, Calvin's various works are peculiarly fitted to restore amongst us a respect for what is holy. We learn from them to grasp in its wholeness the meaning of reality, to avoid materialising it by gluttony and greed, and to be careful not to succumb to the temptation of prostituting it to all the creatures which fill the cosmos, as do the 'enlightened', the theosophists, those who probe the occult, and the gnostics.

We also find in them this imperious rule laid down for the believing man, that no matter how favoured he is by grace, he must not try to pursue a solitary path, for that can only end in utter spiritual disaster. If, on the other hand, he wants to respond to all the demands of his calling, he must take his share in the life and activities of a true Christian community which has the marks of the Gospel, in which all the members being sinners justified by the undeserved goodness of God, human creatures with no merit they can call their own, accept the discipline of submitting their emotions, their thoughts, their principles, their repentance, their miseries, each moment of their lives to the unforeseeable judgment of Holy Scripture.

Calvin conceived of himself as a trustee of the tradition of the early Church, and constantly referred to Bernard of Clairvaux, Augustine of Hippo, Luther and Melanchthon. In this way he was careful to keep himself from breaking out into any kind of worthless or dangerous doctrinal originality. Yet almost in spite of himself he gave expression in his work to the peculiar characteristics of his own faith when he took his doctrine of the indissoluble union of the believer and Christ at the heart of the Church, and made it the basis of an ethic, active and exacting and productive of good living. Such an ethic has never failed to impose on the Protestants of the West, even on those who show least respect for the discipline of the Church, a manner of life and of thought that has no equal.

PRESBYTERIANISM

All his life, Calvin sought to avoid subjecting the Word of God to a logical and rigid system of dogma. Such an achievement would have been of the devil. Moreover, he hated it when men looked to him, sinner that he was, as to an absolute authority. He would have disapproved, therefore, of any attempt to apply the name Calvinist to the Christian communities who followed his teaching in their confessions and whose Church organization was copied from that which he had set up in Geneva. Personally, I feel that it is more fitting to give them the name suggested by their form of government: Reformed Presbyterian Churches.

From the time of their origin these Churches have assumed certain characteristics which have remained as their distinctive features since the sixteenth century. They give the sacraments a place as the means whereby the faithful who receive them with trembling confidence can find the strength and gifts to fulfil their calling and to further their sanctification. They do not believe that God has abdicated in their favour His liberty to work where and when He wills, and that He is therefore bound to use them as intermediaries when He wants to bestow on men the means of salvation. But they do not, for all that, consider that those who believe have any freedom to refuse the continual help that the Church offers them. They hold that, in order not to weaken the power of their preaching, and so that the sacraments which they celebrate shall confirm the faith of their flocks, they must examine themselves and submit themselves to constant reformation and impose on those under their charge the most strict discipline. They take care that such discipline is not purely repressive but such as to effect the cure of sick souls. They claim that their organization and their stability are not the product of the circumstances of any historical situation but spring directly from the priesthood of Jesus and the gifts of the Holy Spirit as those are both set forth and unfolded in Holy Scripture.

'I approve', writes Calvin, 'of those human constitutions

only which are founded on the authority of God, and derived from Scripture, and are therefore altogether divine.'[110]

Though not so foolish as to try slavishly to reproduce all the features of the early Apostolic Church, the Churches which make use of the teaching of Calvin in their tradition at least strive as the primitive Church did, to single out in their midst and to ordain various ministries which are given their recognition. Amongst these offices are pastors, doctors, elders and deacons. They take it for granted that it is Christ by His Spirit who bestows on each of them the gifts necessary to fulfil their function, but they make it a rule that the whole congregation of the faithful by regular and lawful election should in some way humbly ratify what has already been the choice of the Holy Trinity. Although in these four ministries they set up a hierarchy—yet not a harshly strict one—they take pride in the doctrine of the priesthood of all believers and abolish, as incongruous, all distinction between clergy and laity. Through the pastors, doctors, elders and deacons, they carry out their four tasks appointed by God; the ministry of word and sacrament, teaching, discipline and service. They recognize the sole authority of the Old and New Testaments, the truth of which is attested by the internal witness of the Holy Spirit, and they claim for themselves no right in their teaching to do other than enunciate, proclaim and expound the teaching of Scripture in order the better to defend it against those who disparage it.

Besides, the very idea of a theocratic government is regarded by them as the fruit of a tragically perverted way of thinking and is utterly abhorrent to them—though malicious people have accused them of this heresy. They deplore the fact that Zwingli merged Church and State together, and that Luther made the Church too much subject to the State. They desire to see everywhere set up a restricted but frank collaboration between the two powers. The duty of the one is to give clear witness to all regarding the demands of the Word of God, while the other guarantees freedom for such preaching.

As early as the middle of the sixteenth century many Reformed Presbyterian Churches inspired in their study of the text of the Bible by the method and spirit of Calvin, united in faith and in their discipline and ritual, took root in Poland, in Bohemia, in Hungary and above all in the countries of Western Europe. In spite of powerful civil and religious opposition they sprang up and thrived in the French-speaking cantons of Switzerland, in the French provinces of the west, the south, the centre, and the south-east, in the states bordering on the Rhine, in the Low Countries, in the Friesian Isles, in England, Scotland and Ireland. In the seventeenth century they swarmed into South Africa, and the English colonies of America. At the present time there is actually no country in the world where they are not represented. They have always remained conscious of their essential unity and of their common origin. They form a group in the World Presbyterian Alliance, which regularly meets in conference and claims very rightly to have the marks of oecumenicity, of true catholicity.

CONTROVERSIES

In the course of the centuries their teachers have presented Calvin as one to be revered but they have not always managed to avoid, with regard to him, the sin of idolatry. Some of them have reduced the thought of their master to a hardened formal system, void of evangelical content, and then with a strange presumption they have given to its articles the absolute authority of revealed dogma. Having set up in this way an arbitrary standard of orthodoxy they have not hesitated to abuse as dangerous heretics whoever amongst the membership or the ministry did not subscribe to it. This was the beginning of a controversy which, in setting against each other groups of believers belonging to two different religious outlooks, has perpetuated itself to the present day, and is a testimony to the unfailing vitality of the Reformed and Presbyterian Churches.

Calvin was proudly concerned to keep what is holy free from all admixture or defilement. To this end he modestly and discreetly defended his ideas about double predestination, and never ceased to express his disapproval of the mystical expedients by which man is encouraged to over-estimate his own

99

Arminius, guardian of human free-will

powers, and to try to break through the limits set for him in his fallen state and to lay hands himself upon the title deeds of his own salvation in a way that violates their sanctity. He insisted, in short, on the absolute efficacy of divine election.

One of the scholars of the Church of the Netherlands, Jacques Arminius (1560–1609) at the beginning of the seventeenth century, although he professed a real respect for the Calvinistic gospel, sought to modify it in such a way that man's freedom might be to some extent safeguarded. He held that no human creature could ever become entirely dispossessed of his free will. Arminius gave assent to the doctrine that grace was necessary for adoption, justification, sanctification and confirmation, but he affirmed equally that it does not impose itself irresistibly on the human will which, even if reduced to its own resources, can always find within itself the ability to resist grace. Thus on the one hand he assented to the Roman Catholic opinion of pre-destination and grace, and on the other hand found himself in agreement with the Pelagians on the way in which grace acts.

He found a stubborn opponent in his colleague François Gomarus (1563–1641). To avoid committing offence against the majesty of God, the latter took a most extreme interpretation of the sections of *The Institutes* that bear on the subject, and affirmed that original sin and the fall of Adam's posterity are included in God's eternal decree of election in the same way as is redemption itself. Thus it is that, in his view, regeneration is the result of a process which deprives the will of man of all free-dom to decide whether to be converted or not. Besides, in the working out of this deep mystery the will of man is not merely stirred up by God into activity; it, rather, acts so completely under divine impulsion that the new man, knowing and feeling that he entrusts himself to his Saviour through love, believes and repents.

Arminianism was solemnly condemned on 23 April, 1619, during the 135th and 136th sessions of the Synod of Dort which brought together representatives of the main Reformed and Presbyterian Churches. Yet the religious posterity of Arminius, who boasted of his moralistic liberalism, still forms an important party within the Churches to this day. Although it is accused of doing so, this section of the Church does not always go to the extremes of Socinianism, nor does it always empty the sacra-ments of their reality, but it recognizes—no doubt wrongly—in the principle of free thought the cause behind the Reformation.

Opposed to this host of liberals—whom Calvin might per-haps have called Libertines—there are the orthodox, the disciples of Gomarus who, freed from all excessive scrupulosity by the principles of their very strict theology, considered the moralism of their adversaries as the price they had to pay for slackness and loose thinking in matters of doctrine.

If the liberals, then, in their exposition of Calvin are to blame for attenuating his meanings without any compensating re-inforcement, the orthodox are equally so for hardening them to such a degree as to rob them of all living force. During the last thirty years an increasingly important number of members of the Reformed and Presbyterian Churches, desirous of avoiding both these dangers, have tried to study *The Institutes* and the con-nected treatises in a spirit that avoids idolatry, but is evangelical as well as critical.

Contrary to both liberals and orthodox, their view is that theology takes up each system of philosophy and transfigures and replaces it, for it is alone in having the power to fulfil all the functions of philosophy since sin has deprived man of the natural light of his mind. Persuaded that all correct Christian thinking must have this transcendent aspect, and following a lead given by Auguste Lecerf (1872–1943) of France, and Karl Barth of Basle, they are careful not to invest even the person of Calvin with an apostolic or, indeed, prophetic authority. They do not set Geneva over against Rome as two centres radiating opposing influences. The way of obedience which the reformer from Picardy points out to them can be followed if they think less of obeying him and more of submitting themselves to the One who has constrained him to obedience. They recognize that the special characteristic of all the writings that come from his pen is the way they seek to constrain the reader to veritable asceticism in the discipline of thought, to an effort of personal re-flection on the affirmations to which he gives expression. Karl Barth, who represents the most vital movement of thought in the Reformed and Presbyterian Churches of today describes the substance of Calvin's theology in a striking way:

Without any attempt at a complete summary, I find in it a truly majestic insistence on magnifying the sovereignty and providence of God, the source of all reality; a sober and pene-trating judgment on the greatness and feebleness of man, on his nature, his condition, his history and his possibilities; an account at the same time both enthusiastic and solemn of the vicissitudes of the life of the Christian with God; a strong sense of the Church and of what befits it; a supreme horror of all hollow speculation, such as all activity without thought, or the converse; a royal love of the active life, of the depths and the secrets we can discover each day of its course; a skill in holding together both the part of God and the part of man in Christianity, in taking account of the spiritual life and of politics, liberty and discipline, the Church and the State in their essential differences as in their essential correlations; the recognition, finally, that all our strength here below is given to us from on high.[111]

This statement could be subscribed to by the thousands who, throughout the world, find strength by meditating on the analysis to which Calvin submitted the elements of theological reality. It gives us an up-to-date picture of the state of mind and heart of this Calvinistic tradition, which in spite of many misunderstandings, many excesses, much opposition, continues to form the decisions and the thought of a large section of the Christian community.

CATECHISME

C'EST A DIRE LE FORMV-
laire d'inſtruire les enfans en la Chreſtien
té, faict en maniere de dialogue, ou le Mi-
niſtre interrogue, & l'enfant reſpond.

PAR IEHAN CALVIN.

ALTVM SAPERE NOLI

L'Oliue de Robert Eſtienne.

M. D. LIII.

EPHES. II.

Le fondement de l'Egliſe eſt la doctrine des Prophetes, & des

Texts

Calvin's Cure of Souls: Consolation for the Dying

Calvin felt the urgency of his call to be an attentive father-in-God to people of every rank who trusted him with the direction of their conscience, indeed of their earthly affairs, and he never ceased to respond to it zealously. He liked helping them to become their true selves, so that they could offer their Lord a reasonable service. Engrossed as he was with looking after his own health and the general bustle of his church administration, he set apart several hours each day in order to try to solve the difficulties of every kind that were presented to him by the faithful who had recourse to his advice. Often he had to reprimand them, but he anxiously saw to it that his sharpest rebukes were aimed at bringing them back again to the serenity of the peace of God. He who ceaselessly made his own substantial hope of a beatified life more and more a part of himself, strove, whenever the need arose, to assist them to go through death in a manner befitting their own character. When the dying sought his help, Calvin, tireless in his efforts, strove to bring back to their mind the religious precepts and particular rules they had followed while gradually their existence was flowing towards eternity. And thus with a good grace, they would find it possible to answer the summons of their God to appear before Him with all the gains of a life spent in improving their inborn talents. The Lord whom Calvin evoked at the bedside of the dying was not an imperious irritable judge, but a divine friend full of grace and mercy, the slain lamb who takes the place of His unworthy creature to suffer for him. When Anne de Normandie, the wife of Laurent de Normandie, his dear friend, was approaching, tragically young in years, her last hour on earth, he did not leave her even for a moment. He tried to alleviate her grief and anguish by words of counsel that were both sober and intimate. He strengthened himself in forcing himself to uphold her. Here is the account he gives of his peaceful yet sad experience to a friend of the deceased. It will be noticed that he avoids taking pride in his success in this case, for he knows himself only as the unprofitable servant of a kindly and compassionate Master.

Madam, although the news which I am sending you is sad, and must also bring grief to him to whom I beg you to tell it, nevertheless I hope this will not make my letters unwelcome to you.

It has pleased my God to take from the world the wife of my dear brother, Monsieur de Normandie. Our comfort is that He has gathered her to Himself, for, as if He had visibly held out His hand to her, He guided her to the very last sigh. Now since her father must be told about it, we thought that there would be no way more fitting than to ask you if you would kindly go to the trouble of inviting him to see you so that through your being the means of it, his sorrow may be softened. What the gentleman has written to us who recently presented our letters to you, has emboldened us to take this step. He told us that you had introduced the good man in question to the right way of salvation and had given him a taste of the pure and sound teaching to which we must hold. Thus we do not doubt that you are ready to continue your good work even in face of a need such as this. For we could not be better employed than in carrying this message in the name of God to comfort him to whom you already have done so much good, that he may not be grieved beyond what is bearable. Well, Madam, I shall leave it to you to put to him the arguments and reasons which you know are helpful for exhorting to patience. Only I shall briefly tell you the history. It will give you ample material for such an approach to him as will give him cause to be thankful. And according to your prudence and to the grace which God has given you, you will be able to draw from it whatever you think can meet his need.

Having heard of the illness of the good woman we were astonished at how she had been able to stand up so well to the stress of the journey, for she arrived quite fresh and showing no signs of weariness. Indeed she was ready to acknowledge that God had helped her in a remarkable way during that time. Considering her state of health, she kept quite well until shortly before Christmas. Nevertheless the desire and zeal that she had to hear the Word of God upheld her till the month of January. She then began to take to her bed not because it was by now thought that the illness was mortal, but in order to avoid the danger that might otherwise develop. At all events, while expecting a happy outcome and hoping to recover her health, she prepared herself, nevertheless, for death, often saying that if this was not the final blow, it could not be long delayed.

As for remedies, everything possible was done. And if she was cared for as to her bodily comfort, that which she prized most of all was not wanting, namely, pious admonitions to confirm her in the fear of God, in the faith of Jesus Christ, in patience and hope of salvation. For her part, she always showed clearly that all this was not in vain, for in all her own conversation you could see that she had the whole matter deeply impressed on her heart. In short, throughout the whole course of her illness, she proved herself a true sheep of our Lord Jesus Christ, allowing herself to be peacefully led by this great shepherd.

Two or three days before her death, as her heart was more lifted up to God, she spoke with more earnest conviction than ever. Even the day before, as she was exhorting her people, she said to the manservant that he must be careful never to go back to where he had polluted himself with idolatry, and since God had brought him into a Christian Church he must see that he lived a holy life within it. The following night she was oppressed by constant and severe pains. Yet never did one hear any other cry from her than the prayer to God that He might have pity and that He might deliver her from this world, giving her grace always to persevere in the faith which He had given to her.

Towards five o'clock in the morning I went to her. After she had listened very patiently to the teaching, such as the occasion called for, which I set before her, she said:

'The hour draws near. I must depart from the world. This flesh asks nothing more than to go away into corruption. But I hold to the certainty that my God is withdrawing me into His Kingdom. I know what a poor sinful woman I am, but I place my trust in His goodness, and in the death and passion of His Son. Thus I have no doubt of my salvation, since He has assured me of it. I go to Him as to a father.'

While she was speaking in this tenor, a goodly number of people came in. From time to time I interjected a few remarks as seemed to fit the occasion. We also offered prayers to God as the urgency of her need demanded. After having shown afresh how conscious she was of her sins so that she could ask pardon for them from God, and how sure she was of her salvation since she put her trust only in Jesus and took refuge in Him alone, quite on her own impulse she began to recite the *Miserere* as we sing it in the Church, and continued with a loud and strong voice, not without great difficulty, but she pleaded to be allowed to continue. At this point I gave her a short summary of the argument of the Psalm, seeing the pleasure she took in it. Afterwards she took me by the hand and said:

'How happy I am, and how beholden I am to God for having led me here to die! If I had been in that wretched prison, I would not have dared to open my mouth to make confession of my Christianity. Here, I not only have freedom to glorify God, but I have so many helpful arguments to confirm me in my salvation!'

Sometimes she indeed said: 'I am not able for more . . .'

When I replied to her: 'God is able for you. He has indeed shown you until now, how He looks after His own.'

She said immediately: 'I believe it and He makes me feel His help.'

Her husband was there, striving to be brave in such a way that while we all felt sorry for him he amazed us by his fortitude. For, carrying such a grief, as I know, and weighed down by extreme anguish, he had so taken hold of himself as to exhort his better half as freely as if they had to make a truly joyful journey together.

The conversation which I have related took place in a period of great torment which she endured from pains in the stomach. About nine or ten o'clock they abated. Meanwhile, being more relaxed, she did not cease to glorify God, constantly humbling herself to seek her salvation and all her well-being in Jesus Christ.

When speech failed her, she did not cease, however, to tell us by the expression on her face how intent she was as much on the prayers as on the exhortations which one gave. Otherwise she was so still, that it was only her eyes that gave her the appearance of being alive. Towards the end, thinking that she had passed away, I said:

'Now let us pray God that He might give us grace to follow her!'

As I raised myself, she turned her eyes on us, as if charging us to continue to pray, and to comfort her. After that we could see no movement. She died peacefully as if she had fallen asleep.

I pray you, Madam, to excuse me if I have taken too long. For I thought that the father would be much better reconciled if he were fully informed of everything, as if he himself had been on the spot. And I hope that for so good a work you will find nothing troublesome. When Saint Paul speaks about love, he does not forget that we ought to weep with those who weep, that is to say, that if we are Christians we ought to have such compassion and sorrow for our neighbours that we willingly take part in their tears so that we can comfort them as much. It cannot otherwise be, then, that the good man should at first be wrung with grief. Nevertheless he must have been prepared for long now to receive the news, considering that the sickness had already gained such a hold on his daughter that any recovery was despaired of. But the great consolation is the example which she has shown to him and to us all of yielding ourselves to the will of God.

Thus since she has offered herself so peacefully to death, let us follow her in this, acquiescing in what God has done with her, and if her father loved her, let him declare his love in conforming to the desire she had to be submissive to God. And seeing that her end has been so happy, let him rejoice in the grace which God gave to her, which surpasses all the good things we could have in this world.

And now, Madam, having humbly commended myself to your kind favour, I beseech our good God to be always your

Protector, to increase you in all spiritual blessings, and to use you to glorify His Name even to the end.

This 29th of April, 1549,

your humble servant and brother

CHARLES D'ESPEVILLE*[112]

Calvin's Cure of Souls: Exhortation to the Martyrs

Since he lived at a time when the Protestant faith was fanatically repressed and openly persecuted, Calvin had to engage unceasingly in the fearful task of preparing the confessors of their faith for the agonies of their supreme sacrifice. He recalled the famous saying of a Father of the Church that the blood of the martyrs is the seed of the Church. *Also, in his urgent challenge to them not to faint, he had a twofold purpose: to fortify them against the temptation to despair and to make them aware of the precaution they ought to take to make the more effectual their witness with their blood.*

In the month of April 1552, five young theologians—Martial Alba, Pierre Escrivain, Charles Faure, Pierre Navihères and Bernard Seguin—were denounced by a hired agent and thrown into gaol under the authorities of Lyons. The Protestant cantons of Switzerland made repeated and most diplomatic efforts to save them. It was in vain. When all hope of saving them from the flames seemed lost, Calvin made no attempt to soothe them with disparaging illusions, and addressed them in the following letter a few days before their death (16 May, 1553).

My dear brothers,

We have at last heard why the herald of Berne did not return that way. It was because he did not receive the kind of reply that we had so much desired. For the King has refused point-blank all the requests made by the Messieurs of Berne as you will see from the copy of the letters. This means that nothing more is to be looked for from that quarter.

* Charles d'Espeville was Calvin's pseudonym adopted during his stay at Angoulême and his journey in Italy (1534–6).

Indeed, wherever we look here below, God has blocked our path. But there is this consolation, that we can never be frustrated in the hope we have in Him and in His holy promises. You have always rested on this foundation, even at those times when it seemed likely that you would be helped by men—as we thought too. Yet, whatever the prospect has been that you would escape by human means, your eyes have never been so dazzled as to divert either your affection or your trust either in one direction or another.

But now your plight demands more than ever that you should turn your whole mind heavenward. We do not yet know what the outcome will be. But since it seems that it is God's will to make use of your blood to attest His truth, you can do no better than to prepare yourselves for this, beseeching Him so to subdue you to His good pleasure that nothing will hinder you from following wherever He calls you. For you know, my brothers,

Martyrdom of Jean Bonniel at Lille
(Sketch by a Registrar, 1569)

that we must be mortified in order to be offered to Him as a sacrifice.

It cannot otherwise be than that you should undergo fierce conflicts in order that what was said to Peter might be accomplished in you, that they shall carry you whither you would not. But you know in what strength you can fight—a strength on which no one has ever relied and found himself daunted, far less confounded.

And so, my brothers, take heart that you will be strengthened according to your need by the Spirit of our Lord Jesus so that you will never faint under the load of temptations, however heavy it be, any more than He did who won over it the victory so glorious that it is to us an unfailing pledge of our own triumph in the midst of our miseries.

Since it pleases Him to use you even to the extent of death in maintaining His cause, He will lend you a strong hand so that you can fight well, and He will not let one drop of your blood be in vain. And though the fruit may not appear all at once, in time it will surely show itself more abundantly than we can express. But as He has accorded you the privilege that your bonds have been renowned and that they have been noised everywhere abroad, it must happen that in spite of Satan your death should resound far more powerfully so that the name of our good God be magnified thereby.

For my part, I have no doubt, that if it please this kind Father to take you to Himself, that He has preserved you until now, so that your long imprisonment might be a work of preparation, after which He can more effectually awaken those whom He has determined to influence by your death. For, although enemies may do their worst, they will never be able to bury the light which God has made to shine in you so that men can look at it from far off.

I shall not offer you sympathy nor give you any further lengthy exhortations, knowing that the heavenly Father makes His own consolations real and precious to you, and that you take good care to meditate on what He sets before you in His Word. He has already made so clear to us the effect of His indwelling strength in you that we are well assured He will perfect you to the end.

Leaving this world is not for us an affair of chance. You know this, not only because of the certainty you have that there is a heavenly life, but also because you are assured of the gratuitous adoption of our God and you go there as to your inheritance. That God should have ordained you to be His Son's martyrs is a work of superabundant favour. There now remains the conflict to which the Holy Spirit exhorts us not only to go, but even to run. It is a hard and sore trial to see the pride of the enemies of truth so overweening without being checked in any way from above, and their rage so unbridled without God interfering for the relief of His own people. But when it is brought to our mind that our life is hid, and that it befits us to resemble the dead, we then remember that this is not a doctrine just for one day but for all time, and we will not find it strange that our afflictions continue. While it pleases God to give His enemies rope for so long, our duty is quietly to hold ourselves in, though the time of our redemption tarries. Moreover, if He has promised to be the judge of those who have enslaved His people, let us not doubt that there is a fearful punishment waiting for those who have despised His Majesty with a pride so enormous, and have cruelly persecuted those who have purely called upon His name.

Put in practice, then, my brothers, that precept of David's, that you have not forgotten the law of the Lord, although you hold your life in your hands as something to be parted with at any moment. And since He employs your life in a cause so worthy as that of bearing witness to the Gospel, do not doubt that it is precious to Him. The time is near when the earth shall uncover the blood which has been hidden, and we, after being divested of these frail bodies, shall be completely restored. However, let the Son of God be glorified by our shame and let us be content with this testimony, that it is because we hope in the living God that we are persecuted and blamed. In this we have wherewith to despise the whole world and its pride till we are gathered into that everlasting Kingdom where we shall fully enjoy the blessings which we now possess by hope.

My brethren, after humbly recommending myself to your prayers, I pray the good Lord to have you in His holy keeping, to strengthen you more and more by His power, to make you feel what care He takes for your salvation and to increase in you the gifts of the Spirit so that they can serve His glory to the very end.

Geneva, May 1553.

Your humble brother,

JOHN CALVIN

I do not make special remembrance to any particular one of our brethren, because I believe that this letter will be common to all. Up to now I have put off writing to you owing to the uncertainty of your state, fearing lest I might cause you unnecessary anxiety. I pray anew that our good Lord may have His hand stretched out to confirm you.[113]

18th Century tile, found on the roof of an old Huguenot house

Calvin's Ethics

The following paragraphs are from chapters VIII, IX and X of Book III of The Institutes *(final edition). These chapters have had an influence on men of the reformed faith more living, direct and lasting than any other part of Calvin's writings. They have determined for Western Protestantism, down to the least detail, its attitude to the business of living. Those who are merely curious, and do not understand how Calvin's dialectical analyses work out, are baffled by the outlook expressed here, and they do not hesitate to brand the Presbyterians of the Calvinist tradition as inconsistent or indeed hypocritical. But, in fact, what the latter find in Calvin is a satisfying doctrine—an austere and moderate asceticism, tempered by an underlying humanism. On the one hand, in order to train themselves to self-denial and to offering themselves to God in a sacrifice of repentance or amendment, far from seeking to avoid the crosses which are their lot in the midst of the calamities of this earthly life, they are always ready, when these occur, to welcome them with a kind of gratitude, looking on them as the inevitable means by which they can attain to the future life and its splendours. On the other hand, far from shutting themselves off in a mystic withdrawal which would involve them in despising what belongs to this visible world, they make diligent use of the benefits of the present life with sobriety, enjoyment and gratitude, accepting them as lawful and pleasant remedies which God Himself carefully prepares for them in order to alleviate the hardness of existence. Thus they live in a perpetual state of mortified cheerfulness, which is bound to be misunderstood as an offensive act of mummery by those who have no grasp of the principles behind it.*

ON BEARING THE CROSS, WHICH IS ONE PART OF SELF DENIAL

1. The man of faith must lift up his heart even higher so that he comes to where Christ leads His disciples when He calls on each one of them to 'take up his cross' (Matt. 16: 24). For all whom the Lord has adopted and honoured with His fellowship must prepare for a life that is hard and laborious, and full of

'*He began to take this course with Christ, His first-born . . .*'

troubles and many different kinds of evil. This way of putting
His people through such experience in order to test them, is the
will of our Heavenly Father. He began to take this course with
Christ, His first-born, and He pursues it in the case of all His
children. For although that Son was beloved to Him above all
others, the Son in whom He was always well pleased (Matt.
3: 17; 17: 5), yet we see that He was never indulged or given
gentle treatment. Indeed we may say that not only was He subjected continually to a cross while He dwelt on earth, but His
whole life was nothing else than a kind of perpetual cross. The
reason for this is given by the Apostle: He had to learn obedience

116

by the things which He suffered (Heb. 5: 8). Why then should we exempt ourselves from the condition to which Christ our Head had to submit Himself, especially since He submitted Himself in that way for our sakes in order to give us in His own person an example of patience? For this reason the Apostle teaches that all the children of God are destined for this purpose, that they might be made conformable to Him (Rom. 8:29). Hence it is a source of great comfort to us when in the midst of those hard and bitter circumstances which are usually deemed evil and adverse, we have fellowship with the sufferings of Christ in such a way that as He passed through a labyrinth of many evils into heavenly glory, so we too are led to the same destiny through various tribulations (Acts 14: 22). For St Paul himself teaches us in another place that when we experience in ourselves the fellowship of His sufferings we apprehend at the same time the power of His resurrection, and when we are rendered conformable to His death we are thus prepared to share in His glorious resurrection (Phil. 3: 10). How powerfully should this soften all the bitterness of the cross! For it means that the more we are afflicted by adversity, the more firmly we are assured of our fellowship with Christ, and when we have such fellowship with Him, our sufferings are not only blessed to us but are thus used powerfully in the furtherance of our salvation.

2. Moreover, whereas our Lord had no need to undertake to bear His cross, except to testify and prove His obedience to the Father, there are many reasons which make it necessary for us to live our lives constantly under the cross. Firstly, we are too inclined by nature to attribute all our achievements to our own flesh. Unless, therefore, our weakness is demonstrated to our eyes we easily over-estimate the worth of our virtue and imagine that, whatever our circumstances, it will stand invincible against all difficulties. Hence we are apt to become uplifted through what is simply a stupid and inane confidence in the flesh, and the result of this is that we grow proudly independent of God Himself as if our own powers could enable us to do without His grace. The best way for Him to shatter all such arrogance is to

prove to us by experience not only how foolish we are, but also how weak. Therefore He afflicts us with disgrace or poverty or bereavement or disease or other calamities, and when we find that we are unable any longer to bear up under them by our own strength we soon give in. And thus in our humiliation we learn to look to Him for the power which alone can make us strong under the burden of our suffering. This applies even to the most sanctified of men, for no matter how much they may be aware that they depend not on their own strength but entirely on the grace of God, yet they would always feel too confident in their own power and constancy unless they were led through such an experience of the cross to a more thorough knowledge of themselves. Even David was overtaken by this kind of stupidity. 'In my prosperity I said, I shall never be moved. Lord, by thy favour thou hast made my mountain to stand strong; Thou didst hide thy face and I was troubled' (Psalm 30: 6–7). He confesses that prosperity had dulled and blunted his feelings so that, losing all concern for the grace of God on which alone he should have depended, he leant on himself and promised himself lasting stability. If this happened to such a great Prophet, which of us should not fear and be on our guard? Nevertheless those who flatter themselves with ideas of their great constancy and steadiness when things are going well with them come to know that all this is hypocrisy when they are humbled by hard circumstances. This is the way, I say, in which the faithful must come to be made aware of their diseases and learn lessons in humility and get rid of all their perverse confidence in the flesh in order to give themselves recourse to the grace of God. And in such recourse they experience the presence of the divine power in which they have more than sufficient strength.

3. This is what St Paul teaches when he says that tribulation works patience and patience experience (Rom. 5: 3–4). The promise of God to His people, that He will be with them in tribulations, they experience to be true when, supported by His hand, they endure patiently—which they could never do by their own strength. Patience, then, is a proof to the saints that God in reality gives the help He has promised whenever there is need.

In this way also their hope is confirmed, for it would be gross ingratitude not to expect that for the future the truth of God will be what they have already found it, constant and immovable. We see now how many advantages flow in one constant stream from the cross. For, in overturning the overweening opinion we form of our own virtue, and unmasking our hypocrisy which seduces us with its delights, it drives out our pernicious carnal confidence. Having thus humiliated us, it teaches us to recline in God alone so that we are neither overwhelmed nor lose courage. This victory is then followed by hope, in as much as our Lord by thus standing by His promises, establishes His truth for the future. Surely without any further reasons than these, it is obvious how necessary it is that we should be subjected to the cross. For it is of no little importance that our self-love, which blinds us, should be taken away so that we might become fully conscious of our weakness—so impressed by our weakness that we learn to distrust ourselves; so distrustful of ourselves that we learn to transfer our trust to God; so confident in God with heartfelt trust that by means of His help we persevere victorious to the end, standing in His grace, so that we know Him to be true to His promises; and so assured of the certainty of His promises that our hope is strengthened thereby.

4. The Lord has yet another reason for afflicting His servants: in order to test their patience and train them to obedience. Not that they are able to offer Him obedience except in so far as He Himself gives it, but it pleases Him thus to show and to attest, by striking proofs, the graces with which He has endowed His saints lest they should remain concealed within and unused. Accordingly when He brings out openly the strength and constancy of endurance which He has given to His servants, He is said to try their patience. This gives rise to such ways of speaking as: God tempted Abraham (Gen. 22: 1–12), and took knowledge of his piety from this, that he did not refuse to sacrifice his one and only son. For the same reason Peter (1 Peter 1 : 7) teaches that our faith is proved by tribulation, just as gold is tried in a furnace of fire. But who will say that it is not expedient that so excellent a gift as patience which the believer

has received from his God should be put to use in order to be made sure and manifest? Otherwise it would never be valued according to its worth. But if God Himself has good reason to give occasion for calling forth the virtues with which He has endowed His faithful, so that these do not remain hidden and lying useless and perishing, we see that it is not without cause that He sends afflictions to the saints, since without them their patience could not exist. I say also that by the cross they are trained to obedience, seeing that they are taught by this means not to live according to their own wish, but at the disposal of God. Indeed, if everything took place as they wished it, they would never know what it is to follow God. Seneca, the heathen philosopher, says that it was an old proverb, when anyone was exhorted to endure adversity, to say: 'Follow God'. By this they implied that only then does a man truly submit to the yoke of God, when he willingly gives his back and hand to the rod. But if it is only reasonable that we should prove ourselves in all things obedient to the Heavenly Father, we must not decline to allow Him to train us to obedience by every possible method.

5. Nevertheless we do not see how necessary that obedience is unless at the same time we consider how prone our carnal nature is to throw off the yoke of God immediately it is treated with any gentleness or indulgence. For it happens to it exactly as with refractory horses, who, after being a few days in the stable idle and well fed, afterwards become ungovernable and do not recognize their rider by whom previously they allowed themselves to be controlled. In short, what God complains of in the people of Israel is continually the case with all of us: waxing gross and fat, we kick against Him who reared and nursed us (Deut. 32: 15). The kindness of God should allure us to ponder and love His goodness, but we are so ill-disposed that, instead, we invariably become corrupted by His indulgence. Therefore it is more than necessary for us to be restrained by discipline lest we should break forth into such petulance. For this reason, lest by an over-abundance of wealth we become ungovernable, lest elated by honours we become proud, lest

inflated with other advantages of body, mind or fortune we grow insolent, the Lord Himself intervenes, as He sees fit, subduing and curbing by the remedy of the cross the arrogance of our flesh. This happens in various ways according to what is most salutary for each individual. For, as we do not all labour uniformly under the same disease, so we do not all need the same difficult cure. That is the reason why the heavenly physician exercises some with one kind of cross, others with another kind. He uses harsher remedies with others, His purpose being to ensure health for all. Yet no one is exempt or untouched, because He knows that the whole world, to a man, is sick.

6. We may add that our most merciful Father not only requires to prevent our weakness, but has often to correct our past faults in order to keep us in due obedience towards Himself. Therefore immediately affliction comes to us, we should call to mind our past life. In this way, without any doubt, we will find some fault that deserves such a punishment. And yet we must not make this recognition of our sin the principal consideration in exhorting ourselves to patience, for the Scripture supplies us with a much better reason, when it says that in adversity 'we are chastened of the Lord, that we should not be condemned with the world' (1 Cor. 11: 32). We must, then, recognize the kindness and mercy of our Father in the very bitterness of our tribulation, seeing that even in this He does not cease to further our salvation. For he afflicts us not to lose or ruin us, but to deliver us from the condemnation of the world. This thought should lead us to what Scripture teaches us elsewhere: 'My son, despise not the chastening of the Lord, neither be weary of his correction: For whom the Lord loveth, he correcteth; even as a father the son in whom he delighteth' (Prov. 3: 11–12). Where we recognize our Father's rod is it not our part to behave as obedient docile sons rather than to resist, imitating desperate men hardened in their wickedness? God would lose us if He did not draw us back to Himself by corrections, when we have fallen off, so that it is rightly said: 'if ye be without chastisement . . . then are ye bastards, and not sons' (Heb. 12: 8). We are, then, most

perverse if we cannot bear Him when He is manifesting His goodwill to us and the care which He has for our salvation. Scripture teaches that the difference between unbelievers and believers is that the former, like slaves of inveterate and deep-seated iniquity, only become worse and more obstinate under the lash; whereas the latter, like freeborn sons, improve themselves in repentance. Let us choose now which of these we want to be. But as I have already spoken of this elsewhere, it is enough to have here touched on it briefly.

7. Our chief consolation, however, is when we suffer persecution for the sake of righteousness. For our thought should then be of the high honour to which God raises us when He gives us the special badges of His own regiment. By persecution for the sake of righteousness, I mean suffering not only for the defence of the Gospel, but also for the defence of righteousness in any form. Whether, therefore, in maintaining the truth of God against the lies of Satan, or in defending the good and innocent against injury from the wicked, we find ourselves with the hatred and anger of the world against us, and our life, fortune and honour endangered, let it not be grievous or irksome to us to devote ourselves thus far to God, nor let us regard ourselves as wretched in that state in which He with His own life has pronounced us blessed (Matt. 5: 10). Poverty, indeed, considered in itself, is misery. So, also, are exile, contempt, imprisonment, ignominy. Finally, death is the utmost of all calamities. But where the favour of God breathes upon us, there is none of these things which may not turn out to our happiness. Let us be contented, then, with the testimony of Christ rather than with the false opinion of the flesh. It will then happen that like the Apostles we will rejoice as often as He counts us worthy to suffer shame for His Name (Acts 5: 41). Why so? If where we are innocent and we have a good conscience we are deprived of our goods by the wickedness of the ungodly, we are no doubt reduced to poverty as men see it, but actually in this way, the riches that we have towards God in heaven are increased. If we are driven from our homes we are received with all the more

welcome into the family of God. If we are vexed and lightly esteemed, we are the more firmly rooted in Christ. If we are held in disgrace and ignominy, we are all the more exalted in the Kingdom of God. If we are slaughtered, entrance is thereby given us to the blessed life. Should it not shame us to set less value on the things on which the Lord has placed such a price, than on the shadowy and evanescent attractions of the present life?

8. Since, then, by such considerations Scripture gives us abundant solace for the ignominy and calamities we have to endure in the defence of righteousness, we are extremely ungrateful if we do not accept them willingly and cheerfully as from the hand of God, especially since this kind of cross is that most appropriate to believers, and the means by which Christ desires to be glorified in us as St Peter teaches (1 Peter 4: 11). But since to the proud and courageous nature it is more bitter to suffer disgrace than a hundred deaths, St Paul expressly warns us that not only persecution but also disgrace awaits us because we trust in the living God (1 Tim. 4: 10). So elsewhere he encourages us by his own example to walk by evil report and good report (2 Cor. 6: 8). We are not, however, required always to have such cheerfulness that we no longer feel any bitterness and grief. There could not otherwise be any patience of the saints in the cross unless they were tortured with pain and distressed by trouble. If there were no hardship in poverty, no pain in disease, no sting in ignominy, no fear in death, where would be our courage and moderation in showing indifference towards such things? But since there is an inherent bitterness in each one of these which naturally eats through to the mind, the believer shows his fortitude if, being tempted by the feeling of such bitterness, and grievously labouring, yet he boldly withstands and struggles. In this he shows his patience, that though sharply stung, he is nevertheless restrained by the fear of God from breaking out into any excess. In this his eager joy manifests itself, that though pressed with sorrow and sadness he finds rest in the spiritual consolation of God.

9. This conflict which believers maintain against the natural feeling of pain, while they study patience and moderation, is very well described by Paul in these words: 'We are troubled on every side, yet not distressed; we are perplexed, but not in despair; persecuted, but not forsaken; cast down, but not destroyed' (2 Cor. 4: 8–9). We see that to bear the cross patiently does not mean becoming completely stupefied and insensible to any feeling of pain, according to the absurd description of the magnanimous man given by the Stoics of old, as someone who, divested of his humanity, was affected in the same way by adversity as by prosperity, by circumstances that are sad as by those that are joyful, or rather, like a stone, was not affected by anything. And what did they gain by this sublime wisdom? They depicted a sham kind of patience such as was never found among men, nor could ever exist. Indeed, by seeking to have a patience too nicely defined they have made it altogether divorced from human life. There is also now amongst Christians a new kind of Stoics who think that it is wrong not only to groan or weep, but even to be sad and anxious. These strange doctrines are usually started by indolent men who, employing themselves more in speculation than in action, can do nothing else for us than beget such fantasies. But for our part we have nothing to do with this iron philosophy which our Lord and Master condemned not only in word but also by His example. For He groaned and wept both for His own and other people's troubles. Nor did He teach His disciples otherwise. 'Ye shall weep and lament', He said, 'but the world shall rejoice' (John 16: 20), and lest anyone should take a perverse meaning out of this, He expressly declares those who weep to be blessed (Matt. 5: 4). And no wonder! For, if all tears are condemned, what shall we think of the Lord Himself, who sweated drops of blood from His body (Luke 22: 44)? If every kind of dread is regarded as unbelief, where will we place that horror which, we read, amazed Him in no small way? If we disapprove of all sadness, how shall we justify Him when He confesses His soul as sorrowful even unto death (Matt. 26: 38)?

'*St. Peter, when it became necessary to glorify God by death*'

10. I wished to say these things to keep good men from despair, lest, through not being able to throw off the natural feeling of grief, they might give up trying to cultivate patience. There can be no other outcome with those who turn patience into stupidity, and a brave and firm man into a block. Scripture, on the contrary, praises the saints for endurance when they

are so afflicted by the harshness of their troubles that they are neither broken nor give in, when they are so stung by bitterness that they are at the same time filled with spiritual joy, when they are so pressed with anxiety that they breathe exhilarated by the consolation of God. Meanwhile that repugnance remains in their hearts, because natural sense shuns and dreads whatever is averse to it, while pious affection tries to obey the divine will, even through these difficulties. This repugnance the Lord expressed when He spoke thus to Peter. 'When thou wast young, thou girdest thyself and walkedst whither thou wouldest: but when thou shalt be old, thou shalt stretch forth thy hands, and another shall gird thee, and carry thee whither thou wouldest not' (John 21: 18). It is not likely, indeed, that St Peter, when it became necessary to glorify God by death, was driven to it unwilling and resisting: in such a case his martyrdom would scarcely have been praiseworthy. But though He submitted with a spontaneous heartfelt consent to what God had ordained, yet since He had not divested Himself of humanity, He was distracted by a double will. When he thought of the bloody death which He was to die, being struck by the horror of it, He would willingly have escaped it. On the other hand, when He considered that it was God who called Him to it, His fear was vanquished and suppressed, and He approached it willingly—and even joyfully. If, therefore, we wish to be disciples of Christ we must take trouble to see that our hearts are filled with such reverence and obedience to God as may tame and subjugate all affections contrary to what He has ordained. In this way it will come about that whatever be the kind of cross which troubles us, in the greatest possible distress of mind, we will firmly retain our patience. Adversities will have their bitterness which will sting us. In the same way, afflicted with disease, we shall groan and be disquieted and long for health; being pressed by poverty, we shall feel the stings of anxiety and sadness. Likewise the pain of ignominy, contempt and other injuries will wound us. When our friends die, we will pay to Nature the tears that are due. But we will always come back to this conclusion: 'The Lord so willed it, let us then follow His will.' Indeed, this thought must suggest itself amidst the pungency of our grief, amongst groans and tears, in order to incline our hearts to bear cheerfully those things on account of which it is thus pained.

11. Since we have derived the chief reason for bearing the cross from consideration of the divine will, we must briefly explain what is the difference between philosophical and Christian patience. There have been very few philosophers who have advanced so far as to understand that men are exercised in affliction by the hand of God, and that we ought in this matter to submit to God. But even those themselves give no other reason than that *so it must be*. But does not this mean simply that we must yield to God because it is in vain to contend against Him? For if we obey God only because it is necessary, provided we can escape, we shall cease to obey Him. But Scripture wants us to consider something very different with regard to the will of God: namely, first justice and equity, and then concern for our salvation. Hence, Christian exhortations of patience are of this nature: whether poverty, or exile, or imprisonment, or shame, or disease, or bereavement, or any such evil affects us, we must think that none of them happens except by the will and providence of God. Moreover, He does nothing that is not ordered with perfect justice. Is it not true that the innumerable sins we commit each day deserve to be chastised more severely and with a heavier rod than His mercy lays upon us? Is it not most fitting that our flesh should be subdued, and be, as it were, accustomed to the yoke so that it does not break out in anger and wantonness through its own desires? Are not the justice and truth of God worthy of our suffering on their account? But if the equity of God is undoubtedly displayed in our afflictions, we cannot murmur or struggle against them without iniquity. Here we no longer hear that frigid refrain of the philosophers, 'Yield, because it is necessary', but a precept full of life and power, 'Obey, because it is unlawful to resist. Bear patiently, because impatience is rebellion against the justice of God.' Then, since nothing seems attractive to us but that which we perceive to be for our own good and salvation, in this

also our merciful Father consoles us by assuring us that in the very cross with which He afflicts us He provides for our salvation. But if it is clear that tribulations are salutary to us, why should we not receive them with calm and grateful minds? In bearing them patiently we are not submitting to necessity but quietly accepting something that is good for us. These considerations, I say, will so affect us that to whatever extent our hearts are contracted by the bitterness which we naturally feel under the cross, to the same extent they will be expanded with spiritual joy. Hence will follow an act of thanksgiving which cannot exist without joy. But if the praise of the Lord and the act of thanksgiving can arise only from a cheerful and gladdened heart, and there is nothing which ought to interrupt these feelings in us, it is clear how necessary it is to temper the bitterness of the cross with spiritual joy.

OF MEDITATING ON THE FUTURE LIFE

1. Whatever be the kind of tribulation with which we are afflicted, we must always consider the end of it to be to accustom us to despise the present life, so that we may be stirred up to meditation on the future life. For since God knows well how much we are inclined by nature to a blind and even brutish love of this world, He employs the most suitable means to draw us back and shake off our lethargy lest in such love we should cling too strongly to it. There is not one of us who would not want to seem to aspire and strive for heavenly immortality throughout the whole course of his life. For we would be ashamed in no way to excel the lower animals whose condition would not be at all inferior to ours if there was no hope left to us of eternity after death. But if you examine the plans, the desires, the undertakings and works of each one, you see nothing in them but what is of the earth. This stupidity arises from our minds being so dazzled with the glare of wealth, power and honours that they can see no further. In short, the whole soul being entangled by the allurements of the flesh seeks its happiness on the earth. In order to deal with this evil, the Lord drives home the lesson of the vanity of the present life by letting

His people unceasingly experience its miseries. Thus, that they may not promise themselves deep and lasting peace in it, he often allows them to be disturbed and molested by wars, tumults, robberies or other injuries. That they may not long with too much eagerness after fleeting and fading riches, or rest in those they already possess, He reduces them to want, now by exile, now by sterility in their lands, then by fire or by some or other means, at least He restricts them to a modest estate. That they may not indulge too much in the pleasure of married life, He either vexes them by the misconduct of their wives, or humiliates them by the wickedness of their children or afflicts them by bereavement. If in all these respects He treats them gently, nevertheless lest they should swell with vain glory or be elated with confidence, He faces them with diseases and dangers, setting clearly before them how unstable and evanescent are all the good things which are subject to mortality. Then indeed we duly gain benefit from the discipline of the cross when we learn that this life, estimated in itself, is restless, troubled, wretched in innumerable ways, and plainly in no respect happy; that all those things that are called its blessings, are uncertain, fleeting, vain, and mixed up with a great deal of evil. From this we conclude that we can seek or hope for nothing here except conflict, that when we think of the crown, we must raise our eyes to heaven. For it is quite certain that our mind never rises seriously to desire and meditate on the future life, unless it has first become imbued with contempt for the present life.

2. There is no middle way between these two things; either the earth must be worth nothing to us, or keep us fettered by an intemperate love of it. Therefore, if we have any regard for eternity we must diligently strive to extricate ourselves from these evil bonds. Moreover, since the present life has many enticements by which to allure us, and a great show of delight, grace and sweetness by which to soothe us, it is of great importance for us to be now and then withdrawn from it lest we should be fascinated by such enticements. For what would happen, I pray you, if we enjoyed here an uninterrupted career of happiness and plenty, when even the constant stimulus of

affliction cannot arouse us sufficiently to realize our misery. It is not only the learned who know that human life is like smoke or a shadow. There is not a more trite proverb among the common people, and since it has been recognized as something most useful to know, they have enshrined it in many well-known expressions. Yet there is no fact which we ponder less carefully or less frequently remember. For we form all our plans as if fixing on immortality on the earth. If a funeral takes place, or if we go amongst the graves in a cemetery, since then we have the image of death present before our eyes, I admit we philosophize admirably on the vanity of life—though it does not always happen in this way, for sometimes these things hardly move us at all—but when it happens, it is a momentary philosophy which vanishes as soon as we have turned our backs, so that not even a vestige of remembrance is left; in short it passes away just like the applause of a theatre at some pleasant spectacle. For, having forgotten not only death but also mortality itself, as if no rumour of it had ever reached us, we sink back into the foolish security of false confidence in terrestrial immortality. If someone meanwhile breaks in with the proverb, that man is but the creature of a day, we indeed confess it to be true, but in such a heedless way that this thought of perpetuity still keeps hold of our minds. Who then will deny that it is of the highest importance to us all, I do not say, to be admonished with words, but to be convinced by every possible experience of the miserable condition of our earthly life, since even when we are convinced we scarcely cease to be struck with base and stupid admiration for it, as if it contained in itself the sum of all that is good? But if it is necessary for God to train us in this way, our duty is to listen to Him when He calls and shakes us from our torpor, so that despising the world, we might aspire with our whole heart to the future life.

3. The contempt which believers should train themselves to feel for the present life, however, must not be of a kind to beget hatred of it, or ingratitude to God. For, although this life is full of every kind of misery, it is nevertheless rightly to be counted

amongst the blessings of God which are not to be despised. Therefore, if we do not recognize the kindness of God in it we are guilty of gross ingratitude towards Him. Especially ought it to be to believers a proof of the goodness of God, since it is wholly destined to promote their salvation. For before He openly shows us the inheritance of immortal glory, God is pleased to manifest Himself as a Father to us by less spectacular proofs: namely the blessings which we daily receive from His hand. Since, then, this life serves to acquaint us with the goodness of God, shall we disdain it as if it had not a particle of good in it? We ought to have such an opinion of it and fondness for it that we regard it as one of the gifts of the divine benignity which are by no means to be despised. Even if the abundant and clear proofs of this which we have in Scripture were lacking, yet nature herself exhorts us to render thanksgiving to God for having brought us forth into its light, granted us the use of it, and bestowed upon us everything we need for its preservation. Moreover, we find a much higher reason if we reflect that here we are being prepared in some way for the glory of the heavenly kingdom. For the Lord has so ordained it that those who are to be crowned finally in heaven, must first battle on this earth so that they may not triumph before they have overcome the difficulties of war and obtained the victory. Another reason, too, must weigh with us: if we begin here to experience in various ways the sweetness of His kindness and His mercies, it is in order that our hope and desire may be whetted to seek after its full manifestation. And after we have come to the conclusion that our earthly life is a gift of the divine mercy, and it is nothing more than our duty gratefully to remember this grace, then it will be time for us to descend to consider its most wretched condition, and thus escape from that excessive fondness for it to which, as has been said, we are naturally prone.

4. In proportion as this improper love diminishes, our desire for a better life should increase. I confess indeed that the soundest judgment was formed by those who thought that the best thing was not to be born, the second best to die early. For since they were destitute of the light of God and of true religion what

could they see in this life that was not threatening and evil? Nor was it unreasonable that those who were sad and wept at the birth of their kindred should have a glad festival at their deaths. But they did this without profit, because they were devoid of the true doctrine of faith, and did not see how that which in itself is neither happy nor desirable can work out for the good of the righteous. Hence their way of thinking led them into despair. Let believers, then, always have this aim in making their estimate of this mortal life: seeing that there is nothing in it but wretchedness, let them devote their whole selves more readily and with few encumbrances to meditating on that future and eternal life. When it comes to a comparison between them, then, not only can the former be passed over carelessly, but in comparison with the latter can be disdained and contemned. For if heaven is our country what can the earth be but a place of exile? If departure from the world is entrance into life what else can the world be but a tomb, and as for remaining in it, what else can that be than being immersed in death? If to be freed from the body is to gain possession of full freedom, what else is the body but a prison? If it is the very summit of happiness to enjoy the presence of God, is it not miserable to be without it? But until we depart from the world, we are absent from the Lord (2 Cor. 5: 6). Thus if the earthly is compared with the heavenly life there is no doubt that it may be lightly despised and trampled under foot. It is true, indeed, that we ought never to hate it except in so far as it keeps us in subjection to sin, and even this hatred cannot properly be directed against life itself. At all events our attitude towards it as regards weariness or hatred should be that while we long for it to end, we are prepared to remain in it as long as it is the Lord's will, so that what weariness we have will be far from murmuring or impatience. For it is as if we were in a post in which the Lord had stationed us and in which we must remain until He recalls us. Paul indeed laments his condition in being bound longer than he would by the fetters of the body, and sighs with ardent longing to be delivered (Rom. 7: 24). Nevertheless in order to be prepared for the will of God, he declared himself ready for one course or another, since he knew that he owed it to God to glorify His Name either by life or by death, and it is for God Himself to determine what is most conducive to His glory (Phil. 1: 23). Therefore if it becomes us to live and die to the Lord, let us leave the period of our life and death to His disposal. Yet let us ardently long for death and constantly meditate upon it, and in comparison with future immortality let us despise life, and, because of the bondage of sin, long to renounce it whenever it shall so please the Lord.

5. But surely it is a strange thing that many who boast of being Christians, instead of thus longing for death, have such a horror of it that as soon as they hear it mentioned they tremble as if it were something wholly ominous and dreadful. It is not to be wondered at if our natural feelings should be shocked when we hear it said that our body is to be separated from our soul, but it is quite intolerable that the light of piety should not so burn in the Christian breast that with the greater consolation it should overcome and suppress that fear. For if we consider that this tabernacle of our body which is unstable, defective, corruptible, fading, pining and putrid is dissolved in order that it may be restored in sure, perfect, incorruptible and heavenly glory, will not faith compel us eagerly to desire what nature dreads? If we reflect that by death we are recalled from exile to inhabit our native, indeed, our heavenly country, shall we derive no consolation from this? But, it may be objected, everything longs for a permanent existence. I admit this, and therefore I maintain that we ought to aspire to future immortality where there prevails a stable condition which appears nowhere on the earth. For Paul admirably teaches believers to hasten cheerfully to death, not 'that we would be unclothed, but clothed upon' (2 Cor. 5: 4). Is it right that the lower animals and the inanimate creatures themselves, even wood and stone, should have some feeling of their present vanity and long for the final day of resurrection that with the sons of God they may be delivered from vanity; while we, on the contrary, endued with the light of intellect and more than intellect, enlightened by the Spirit of God, when we are faced with the question of the meaning of our life, raise our souls no higher than the corruption of

this earth? But it is not my purpose, nor is this the place, to argue against this great perversity. And I protested from the start that I had no wish to engage in a diffuse discussion of common-places. I advise those whose minds are so timid to read the short treatise of Cyprian entitled *On Mortality*, unless they are worthy only to be sent back to the philosophers that by studying what they say on the contempt of death, they may be made to blush. However, we must hold it as fixed that no one has made much progress in the school of Christ except he who looks forward with joy to the day of death and final resurrection. For St Paul distinguishes all believers by this mark (2 Tim. 4: 8; Tit. 2: 13); and it is the habit of Scripture to recall us to this, when it wants to give us a sound reason for rejoicing: 'Look up', says our Lord, 'and lift up your heads; for your redemption draweth nigh' (Luke 21: 28). Is it reasonable, I ask, that what He wished to have the effect of stirring us up to exultation and alacrity, should produce nothing but sadness and consternation? If it happens thus, why do we still glory in Him as our Master? Therefore let us adopt a sounder attitude of mind, and, however repugnant the blind and stupid longing of the flesh may be, let us not hesitate to desire the advent of the Lord not only in wish but even with groans and sighs, as the supreme event of all. He will come to us as a Redeemer who will draw us out of this immense abyss of evil and misery to lead us to the blessed inheritance of His life and glory.

6. This is indeed the case. The whole body of the faithful, as long as they live on earth, must be like sheep for the slaughter (Rom. 8: 36) in order that they may be conformed to Christ their Head. They would therefore be in a most deplorable state if they did not lift up their minds to heaven, in order to rise above all that is in the world and to penetrate beyond the present aspect of affairs (1 Cor. 15: 29). On the other hand, when they have once raised their heads above all earthly objects, though they see the wicked flourishing in riches and honour, enjoying deep peace, indulging in luxury and splendour, and revelling in all kinds of delights, though they moreover should be treated inhumanly by them, suffer insult from their pride, be

robbed by their avarice, or assailed by any other passion, they will have no difficulty in bearing up under these evils. For they will always have before their eyes that day in which God will receive His faithful servants into their rest in His Kingdom,

*'The beggar died, and was carried
by the angels into Abraham's bosom' (Luke 16: 22). Engraving by Abraham Bosse
17th Century*

wipe away all tears from their eyes, clothe them in a robe of glory and joy, feed them with the ineffable sweetness of His pleasures, exalt them to share with Him in His greatness, in short: admit them to participation in His blessedness (Isa. 25: 8; Rev. 7: 17). But the wicked who may have flourished on the earth, He will cast forth in extreme ignominy, will change their delights into horrible torments, their laughter and joy into wailing and gnashing of teeth, will spoil their peace by dire torments of conscience, and punish their luxury with unquenchable fire. He will also put them in subjection to the godly whose patience they abused. For this is justice—as St Paul witnesses— to give rest to those who are miserable and unjustly afflicted, and tribulation to the wicked who afflict the good when the Lord Jesus shall be revealed from heaven (2 Thess. 1: 6–7). This, indeed, is our only consolation. Deprived of it we must either lose courage, or destroy ourselves by finding solace in the vanity of the world. For the Psalmist confesses that he vacillated and that his feet almost slipped when he gave too much attention to the prosperity of the wicked in this present life, and that he found no resting place till he entered the sanctuary of God and considered the latter end of the righteous and the wicked (Ps. 73: 2, 3, 17, etc.). To conclude in a word, the Cross of Christ then only triumphs in the hearts of believers over the devil and the flesh, sin and sinners, when their eyes are directed to the power of His resurrection.

HOW TO USE THE PRESENT LIFE AND ITS COMFORTS

1. In the same elementary way, Scripture also instructs us carefully in the proper use of earthly blessings, a subject which is by no means to be neglected when it is a question of ordering our life well. For if we are to live we must use the necessary supports of life. Nor can we even shun those things which seem rather to serve our pleasure than our need. We must therefore observe due measure that we may use them with a pure conscience whether for necessity or for pleasure. This is what is prescribed by the Lord when He teaches us that to His people the present life is a kind of pilgrimage by which they hasten to the heavenly kingdom. If we are only to pass through the earth, there is no doubt that we ought so to use its blessings that they assist our progress rather than retard it. Accordingly, St Paul

'A kind of pilgrimage by which they hasten to the heavenly kingdom . . .'
Christian Emblems by Georgette de Montenay, 1571

has good reason to warn us that we must use this world as if we were not using it and in buying possessions have the same attitude as if we were selling them (1 Cor. 7: 30–31). But since this is a slippery place, and there is a danger of falling as much into one extreme as into the other, let us fix our feet where we can stand safely. There have been some good and holy men who seeing that intemperance and luxury unless strictly curbed are perpetually carried to excess, and desiring to correct such a pernicious evil, allowed men to use corporeal goods only in so far as was required by necessity. This they did because they could see no other remedy. Their counsel was pious indeed, but they were much too austere. For it is a very dangerous thing to bind consciences in closer fetters than those in which they are bound by the Word of God. For, according to them, necessity meant abstaining from everything which could be done without. Therefore, according to them, it was scarcely lawful to add anything to bread and water. There were others still more austere,

Crates, casting away his riches

as is related of Crates the Theban, who threw his riches into the sea because he thought that if they did not perish, he himself would perish because of them. On the other hand there are many today who, while they seek a pretext for carnal intemperance in the use of external things and wish at the same time to pave the way for licentiousness, take for granted what I by no means concede; that this liberty is not to be modified by any restraint, but that it is to be left to each man's conscience to use them as much as he thinks lawful. I indeed confess that we neither ought nor can bind consciences in this matter by fixed and precise legal formulae, but since Scripture lays down general rules for the legitimate use, we should keep within the limits which they prescribe.

2. Let us begin by stating that we do not err in the use of the gifts of God when we refer them to the end for which their Author created and destined them, since He created them for our good and not for our destruction. No man will keep the true path better than he who shall have this end carefully in view. But if we consider for what end He created food, we shall find that He not only wished to provide for our necessity, but also for our enjoyment and delight. Thus in clothing, besides necessity His aim was to provide what was becoming and honourable. In herbs, trees and fruits besides their various uses, He wishes to rejoice our eyes by their beauty and to give us pleasure in their scent. Were this not so, the Psalmist would not number among the mercies of God that wine rejoices the heart of man, and oil makes his face to shine (Ps. 104: 15). The Scriptures would not mention here and there, in order to recommend His benignity that He had given all these things to men. The natural qualities of things themselves show to what end and how far they may be lawfully enjoyed. Has the Lord adorned the flowers with all the beauty which spontaneously breaks into our sight, and the sweet scent which delights the sense of smell, and shall it be unlawful for us to enjoy that beauty and this odour? What? Has He not so distinguished colours as to make some more agreeable than others? Has He not given qualities to gold and silver, ivory and marble, which make them more precious than other metals or stones? In short, has He not given us many things which we ought to value without their being necessary to us?

3. Have done then with that inhuman philosophy which in allowing no use of the creatures but for necessity not only deprives us of the lawful fruit of the divine beneficence, but cannot be realized without depriving man of all his senses and reducing him to a block. But on the other hand let us no less

ANIMÆ INCVRIA OB NIMIAM CORPORIS CVRAM.

Homo carnalis

diligently guard against the lusts of the flesh which if not held in order burst out beyond all limits. Moreover, there are those who, as I have said, under the pretence of liberty allow themselves every kind of licence. Such lusts must be restrained, in the first place, by this rule: every good thing around us was

The man who indulges the flesh neglects his soul

created so that we might acknowledge their Author and respond to His indulgence with thanksgiving. But where is the thanksgiving if you so gorge or stupefy yourself with feasting and wine as to be unfit for offices of piety or the duties of your calling? Where is the recognition of God if the flesh, boiling forth in lust

141

through excessive indulgence, so infects the mind with its impurity that it cannot discern what is right and honourable? How may we thank God for giving us our clothing if on account of its sumptuousness we both admire ourselves and despise others; if by elegance and splendour we prepare ourselves for unchastity? Where is our recognition of God, if the glare of these things captivates our minds? For many are so addicted to such delights with all their senses that their mind lies buried. Many are so delighted with marble, gold and pictures that they become marble-hearted—are changed as it were into metal and made like painted figures. The kitchen with its savoury smells so engrosses them that they have no spiritual savour. The same thing may be seen in other matters. Therefore it is clear that this consideration means that licentious abuse is to be curbed, and confirms the rule of St Paul that we should make no provision for the flesh to fulfil its lusts (Rom. 13: 14), which, if they are given too much scope, boil over furiously out of control.

4. But there is no surer or quicker way than when we are led to despise the present life and to aspire to celestial immortality. For hence two rules arise: first, that they who use this world ought to be as little affected by it as if they used it not; they who have wives, as if they had none; they that buy as though they possessed not—according to the teaching of Paul (1 Cor. 7: 30–1): secondly, we must learn to be no less placid and patient in enduring penury than moderate in enjoying abundance. He who makes it his rule to use this world as if he used it not, not only cuts off all gluttony in regard to meat and drink, and all effeminacy, ambition, pride, excessive show and austerity in regard to his table, his house and his clothes, but removes every care and affection which might hinder him from turning his thoughts to the heavenly life, or cultivating the interest of his soul. Long ago it was well said by Cato, that luxury causes great care and produces great carelessness as to virtue: and there is an old proverb that those who are much occupied with the care of the body, usually give little care to the soul. Therefore, while the liberty of the Christian in external matters is not to be tied down to a strict rule, it is subject to this law: that he must

indulge as little as possible. On the other hand it must be his constant aim to cut off all show of superfluous abundance, not to speak of curbing luxury, and carefully to beware of making a hindrance for himself out of things that ought to help him.

5. Another rule is, that those in narrow and slender circumstances should learn to bear their wants patiently lest they become immoderate in their desires. Those who observe moderation have made no small progress in the school of Christ, as, on the other hand, he who has made little progress in this matter has scarcely anything to show as a proof that he is a disciple of Christ. For besides the fact that many other vices accompany a longing for earthly good, it happens almost always that he who is impatient under poverty shows a contrary vice in abundance; by this I mean that he who is ashamed of a shabby garment will be vainglorious in a splendid one; he who, not being contented with a slender supper, torments himself with the desire for something better, will intemperately abuse that luxury if he obtains it, he who finds it difficult to submit to a private and humble condition but is unsatisfied in heart will by no means be able to abstain from pride if he attains to honour. Therefore all those who desire to serve God unfeignedly should learn, after the example of the Apostle, both to be full and to be hungry, both to abound and to suffer need (Phil. 4: 12). Scripture, moreover, has a third rule for moderating the use of earthly blessings, on which we briefly touched in discussing the precepts of charity. For it declares that they have all been given to us by the kindness of God, and destined for our use so that we may look on them as a trust of which one day we shall have to give account. We must therefore administer them as if we constantly heard this sentence sounding in our ears, 'give an account of your stewardship' (Luke 16: 2). At the same time let us remember who it is that calls us to account: He who, while He has so highly commended abstinence, sobriety, frugality and moderation, also abominates luxury, pride, ostentation and vanity; who approves of no stewardship of goods but that which is combined with charity; who with His own lips has already condemned all those pleasures which withdraw the heart from chastity and poverty or darken the intellect.

6. The last thing to be observed is that the Lord enjoins each one of us, in all the actions of His life, to have regard to His own calling. For He knows how much the human mind burns with restlessness, with what it is carried away hither and thither, how eager its ambition to hold opposites at one time in its grasp. Therefore, lest all things should be thrown into confusion by our folly and rashness, He has assigned distinct duties to each in the different modes of life. And that no one may lightly overstep his proper limits, He has called such modes of life vocations. Each man's mode of life, therefore, is a kind of station assigned to him by the Lord, that he may not be driven about at random all his life. So necessary is this distinction that in His sight all our actions are estimated by it, and often in a very different way from that in which human reason or philosophy would estimate them. There is no more illustrious deed, even among philosophers, than to free one's country from tyranny, and yet the private individual who stabs the tyrant is openly condemned by the voice of the heavenly Judge. But I am unwilling to dwell on particular examples: it is enough to know that the call of the Lord is the beginning and foundation of all right action. He who does not act with reference to it will never keep the right path in the discharge of his duty. He will be able to make his actions sometimes laudable in appearance, but whatever he may be in the sight of man, he will be rejected before the throne of God, and, besides, there will be no harmony in the different parts of his life. Hence only he who directs his life to this end will have it ordered in the best manner, because he will not dare to attempt more than his calling justifies, nor will he allow himself to be driven by his own rashness, knowing that it is unlawful to go beyond his own bounds. He who is obscure will not decline to cultivate a private life, that he may not abandon the position in which God has placed him. Again, in all our cares, toils, annoyances and other burdens, it will give no small alleviation when each of us knows that God controls all these. The magistrate will more willingly perform his office, and the father of the family will confine himself to his particular

duty; in short, everyone in his own mode of life will, without repining, suffer its inconveniences, cares, uneasiness and anxiety, persuaded that it is God who has laid on the burden. This too will afford us exceptional consolation: that there is not a work so mean or sordid as will not have splendour, and value before God, provided that in doing it we follow our proper calling.

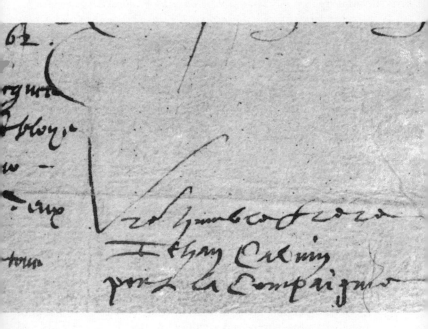

Votre humble frère Jehan Calvin pour la Compagnie

The Calvinistic Doctrine of Art

It is repeatedly affirmed that Calvin marks himself out as different from most of the other reformers by his barbarous iconoclasm. Sensitive rather to the lasting charms of melody and verse than to contemporary fashions, a discriminating lover of poetry and music, he would have launched anathemas against all plastic imagery, as an outrage against the absolute transcendence of the Divine Majesty. In the three aphorisms which follow he expresses his views unequivocally. Regarding the sublime technique of sculptors and painters as the expression of a great divine gift, he does not wish it to be debased by being misdirected to sacrilegious ends. Though he curses every attempt to impose upon the Lord of the Bible a face with recognizable features, he nevertheless considers the cosmos, the sumptuous world around us, as a vast source of elementary themes on which artists have an unquestionable right to exercise their genius and their patience with complete integrity. He urges them, moreover, to think of God as a peerless Creator, to observe the conventions of a moderate realism, and to avoid making any arbitrary alteration, under the specious pretext of improving on them, in the characteristics of the creatures whose likeness they are rendering in such useful ways. Lastly, he takes care not to justify pictures or statues by assigning to them a moral or didactic purpose. He acknowledges that these artistic products can, without doing injury to the stern aspect of the faith, offer to the Christian a means of delight and diversion.

I am not, however, so superstitious as to think that no visible representation of any kind should be tolerated; but since sculpture and painting are gifts of God, what I insist on is that both shall be used purely and lawfully, so that what the Lord has bestowed upon us for His glory and our good shall neither be polluted by preposterous abuse, nor perverted for our destruction.[114]

If we wish to draw the conclusion that it is not lawful to make any picture, that would be a misapplication of what Moses is telling us. There are very simple people who will say, 'It is not lawful to make an image.' That means, painting no image, and not making any portrait. But that is not what the Holy Scripture means, when it is said that it is not lawful to represent God, because He has no body. With men, however, it is quite another thing. What we see can be represented by painting.[115]

It remains to us, then, to paint and to carve only such things as are seen by the eye, in such a way that the Majesty of God, who is above human sight, might not be corrupted by empty fancies that can only insult it. As regards the lawful pursuit of engraving or painting, there are historical incidents to make memorials of, or else a figure or medallion of beast, or town, or country. It can be an advantage for histories to have some notice or remembrance made of them, and as for the other things, I do not know what end is served except that of giving pleasure.[116]

'or else a figure or medallion of beast or town or country.'
Enamel by Bernard Palissy

Early 17th Century Dutch caricature
(Inscription reads, 'The light is placed on the candlestick')

Lutherans and Calvinists

If we ignore some minor points of controversy we may make the assertion that the disciples of Calvin and the followers of Luther while confessing the real presence of Christ in the Eucharist, did not agree among themselves as to the mode of that presence. Called by the Duke of Württemberg to conversations at Montbéliard with accredited representatives of the Lutheran school (1586), Theodore Beza did not succeed in persuading them to join with him in drawing up a formula of concord to which they might unanimously and unreservedly subscribe. Those who may be curious, by studying some of the theses and antitheses of this important colloquy, can learn an interesting yet forceful lesson from the fine doctrinal distinctions inspired by a zeal far too bitter, which separated the doctors who took part in it.

THESIS I OF THE WÜRTTEMBERG THEOLOGIANS

It is agreed that all the faithful eat spiritually the Flesh of the Son of Man and drink His Blood according to the saying of Jesus Christ: 'Except ye eat the flesh of the Son of Man, and drink his blood; ye have no life in you' (John 6: 53). This spiritual manducation takes place by faith, even apart from the use of the Lord's Supper, and is always beneficial. For Jesus Christ speaks thus of it in St John (chap. 6): 'Whoso eateth my flesh, and drinketh my blood, hath eternal life.' As on the contrary, the manducation which takes place in the Lord's Supper is at times harmful and leads to judgment and condemnation. From which it appears that the one is quite different from the other, although spiritual manducation may be necessary for the beneficial reception of the Lord's Supper.

ANTITHESIS I OF THEODORE BEZA

We do not assert any other reception of Jesus Christ, whether through the Word by itself (John 6) or through the Sacraments, as in the institution of the Lord's Supper, than a spiritual reception, that is to say, one which takes place only by virtue of the Holy Spirit and by means of faith. We always acknowledge that what is effected through the bare Word is different from that which is sacramental only with regard to the external form but not as to the thing signified and presented, nor, moreover, as to the reception of the same. For, where the Word alone is concerned God works in us only through the ears, but He adds to the Sacraments something extra, that is, the signs which can be seen and grasped by all our other senses. Whence it happens that if the unworthiness of those who come to the Sacraments puts no obstacle in the way, the sacramental communion is more efficacious and more definite than that which is spiritual only by the hearing of the Word alone.

THESIS V OF THE WÜRTTEMBERG THEOLOGIANS

The question is: to know if the true Body and the true Blood of our Lord Jesus Christ are really and substantially present in the Holy Supper and are also distributed with the bread and the wine, and if this Body and this Blood are taken by mouth, as much by those who come to the Supper unworthily as by those who are worthy, as much by the bad as by the good, by the unbelieving as by the believing, in such a way, nevertheless, that the faithful receive comfort and life in the Supper, and the unfaithful participate there to their judgment and condemnation. We give an affirmative answer to this question.

ANTITHESIS V OF THEODORE BEZA

And we on the contrary give a negative answer. We do not deny, nevertheless, that the true Body and the true Blood of our Lord Jesus Christ are really present to all those who come to the Lord's Supper rightly administered, to be received not by means of the body, but of the soul, not by the mouth, but by means of faith. By which it happens that those who come there unworthily and do not have faith, although the Sacrament in its entirety is presented to them, they nevertheless only receive the signs alone in such a way, however, that they become guilty of the Body and Blood of the Lord, not for having taken such, but for having despised such.

THESIS VI OF THE WÜRTTEMBERG THEOLOGIANS

We do not mean by these words: *in*, *with*, or *under* the bread, anything else than that those who eat the bread and drink the wine in the Supper really receive also in the same measure the Body and the Blood of Christ. And in the same way also these words: *substantially*, *corporally*, *really*, *essentially*, *orally*, do not signify any other thing than the true presence and manducation of the Body and Blood of Christ in the Holy Supper.

ANTITHESIS VI OF THEODORE BEZA

We know very well that the Fathers also used these ways of speaking, but not, however, to prove that the substance of the things signified were *in*, *under*, or *with* the signs in one same place, but to let man understand that the Body and Blood of the

Title page of Beza's Brief Exposition, *1560*

BREFVE EX-
POSITION DE LA
table ou figure côtenát les principaus
poincts de la religion Chrestienne.

Par Theodore de Besze.

bres: parquoy, tout arbre qui ne fait

La coignée est ia mise à la racine des ar-

pas bõ fruit, sera couppé & ietté au feu. Matth:

PAR IEAN RIVERY.
M. D. LX.
Auec priuilege.

Lord were also truly present to the faith of those who present themselves at the Supper, as the words of institution indicate and the outward signs witness to the outward senses. Meanwhile, inasmuch as we perceive that for the foundation of this real consubstantiation, those ways of speaking are drawn from other sources, we avoid such, as being dangerous and less appropriate. And as for the words: *substantially*, *corporally*, *essentially*, if they are applied to things which are given, we regard them as used in their correct sense, but not if they are made to describe the sacramental union or the mode of the presence. We admit also that this word, *really*, taken for *truly*, and used without dissimulation, is not bad. In our opinion, however, these words must be used cautiously. But as for this word: *orally*, like that of the Papists: *sensually*, we completely reject it as being both false in its sense and barbaric in its form.[117]

Theodore Beza

Calvinistic Tradition and Philosophy

Calvin mistrusted philosophers and mystics. He accused them of relying too much on deceptive lights in their vain efforts to penetrate into the hidden darkness of the being of God. Suspecting them of Titanism, he regarded them as rebels, vainglorious beings who, while outwardly keeping up a show of deference, were surreptitiously trying to mount up to heaven to overthrow the Lord and transfer His royalty to man. His immediate followers accepted Aristotelianism, the mental processes of which they judged capable of giving a satisfying account of the nature of the creatures inhabiting the world, nevertheless they had an intense dislike for Platonic gnosis. One philosopher, however, the founder of modern epistemology, Francis Bacon (1561–1626), was fortunate enough to succeed not only in adjusting himself to Calvinistic orthodoxy, to which English theologians were always slow to give approval, but also in finding that through it he could express his personal convictions in such a way that in no sense did he depart from his own habitual originality of expression. His Confession of Faith *meets the demands of the most scrupulous Calvinistic zealots. Yet Francis Bacon could so master the thought of Calvinistic orthodoxy and so adorn its platitudes familiar to the men of his day that he made it the inspiration of a kind of baroque poem which could appeal to the Elizabethans on the same level as their ordinary preoccupations. We can discern here likewise the scrupulous and exacting care of an ardent philosopher to reconcile the never-failing initiative of divine freedom with the inexorable determinism of the laws of nature. This text is worthy of careful study by the modern reader, for in the Calvinistic tradition it marks a signal success, which yet is fraught with many dangers.*

1. I believe that nothing is without beginning, but God; no nature, no matter, no spirit, but one only, and the same God. That God, as He is eternally almighty, only wise, only good in His nature, so He is eternally Father, Son, and Spirit, in three persons.

TERTIUS
OPTICONE
PHILOSOPHIÆ
PRINCEPS

2. I believe that God is so holy, pure, and jealous, that it is impossible for Him to be pleased with any creature, though the work of His own hands; so that neither angel, man, nor world, could stand, or can stand, one moment in His eyes, without His beholding the same in the face of a Mediator; and therefore, that before Him, with whom all things are present, the Lamb of God was slain before all worlds; without which eternal counsel of His, it was impossible for Him to have descended to any work of creation; but He should have enjoyed the blessed and individual society of three persons in Godhead for ever.

3. But that, out of His eternal and infinite goodness and love, purposing to become a Creator, and to communicate with His creatures, He ordained in His eternal counsel, that one person of the Godhead should be united to one nature and to one particular of His creatures; that thus, in the person of the Mediator, the true ladder might be fixed, whereby God might descend to His creatures, and His creatures might ascend to God; so that God, by the reconcilement of the Mediator, turning His countenance towards His creatures, though not in equal light and degree, made provision for the dispensation of His most holy and secret will; whereby some of His creatures might stand, and keep their state; others might possibly fall, and be restored; and others might fall, and not be restored to their estate, but yet remain in being, though under wrath and corruption; all with respect to the Mediator; which is the great mystery and perfect centre of all God's ways with His creatures, which all His other works and wonders but serve and to which they refer.

4. That He chose, according to His good pleasure, man to be that creature, to whose nature the person of the eternal Son of God should be united: and amongst the generations of men, elected a small flock, in whom, by the participation of Himself, He purposed to express the riches of His glory; all the ministration of angels, damnation of devils and reprobates, and universal administration of all creatures, and dispensation of all times, having no other end, but as the ways and ambages of God, to be further glorified in His saints, who are one with their head the Mediator, who is one with God.

Francis Bacon

5. That by the virtue of this His eternal counsel He condescended of His own good pleasure, and according to the times and seasons to Himself known, to become a Creator; and by His eternal Word created all things; and by His eternal Spirit comforts and preserves them.

6. That He made all things in their first estate good, and removed from Himself the beginning of all evil and vanity, leaving it to the liberty of the creature; but reserved for Himself the beginning of all restitution to the liberty of His grace; using, nevertheless, and turning the falling and defection of the creature, which to His prescience was eternally known, to make way for His eternal counsel regarding a Mediator and the work purposed to accomplish in Him.

7. That God created spirits, of whom some kept their standing, and others fell; He created heaven and earth, and all their armies and generations; and gave to them constant and everlasting laws, which we call nature; which is nothing but the laws of the creation.

8. These laws, nevertheless, have had three changes or times, and are to have a fourth or last. The first, when the matter of heaven and earth was created without forms; the second, the period of the perfection of each day's work; the third, by the curse, which nothwithstanding was no new creation; and the last at the end of the world, the manner of which is not yet fully revealed; so that the laws of nature, which now remain and govern inviolably till the end of the world, began to be in force when God first rested from His works, and ceased to create; but received a revocation, in part, by the curse; since which time they change not.

9. That although God has rested and ceased from creating since the first Sabbath, nevertheless He accomplishes and fulfils His divine will in all things, great and small, singular and general, as fully and exactly by providence, as He could by miracle and new creation, though His working be not immediate and direct, but by intermediate means; not violating nature, which is His own law upon the creature.

10. That at the first, the soul of man was not produced by heaven or earth, but was breathed immediately from God; so that the ways and proceedings of God with spirits are not included in nature, that is, in the laws of heaven and earth, but are reserved to the law of His secret will and grace; through which God still works, not resting from the work of redemption, as He rests from the work of creation; but continues working till the end of the world; when that work also shall be accomplished, and an eternal sabbath shall ensue. Moreover, whenever God transcends the law of nature by miracles, which one may look on as new creations, He does this solely as part of His work of redemption, a greater work than that of creation, and to which all God's signs and miracles refer.

11. That God created man in His own image, in a reasonable soul, in innocence, in free-will, and in sovereignty; that He gave him a law and commandment, which was in his power to keep, but he kept it not; that man made a total defection from God, presuming to imagine that the commandments and prohibitions of God were not the rules of good and evil, but that good and evil had their own principles and beginnings, and that he lusted after the knowledge of those imagined beginnings; that he willed to depend no more upon God's will revealed, but upon himself and his own light, as a god; than which there could be no sin more opposed to the whole law of God; that yet, nevertheless, this great sin had not its origin in the malice of man, but was insinuated by the suggestion and instigation of the devil, who was the first defected creature, and fell by his own malice, not by temptation.

12. That upon the fall of man, death and vanity entered by the justice of God; and the image of God in man was defaced; and heaven and earth, which were made for man's use, were subdued to corruption by his fall; but then, that instantly, and without intermission of time, after the word of God's law became through the fall of man, useless as to obedience, there succeeded the greater word of the promise, that the righteousness of God might be wrought by faith.

13. That the law of God as well as the word of His promise endure the same for ever; but that they have been revealed in several manners, according to the dispensation of times. For the law was first imprinted in that remnant of the light of nature which was left after the fall, being sufficient to accuse; then it was more manifestly expressed in the written law; and was yet more opened by the prophets; and, lastly, expounded in the true perfection by the Son of God, the great Prophet, and perfect interpreter, as also fulfiller of the law. That likewise the word of the promise was manifested and revealed; first, by immediate revelation and inspiration; after, by figures, which were of two natures: the one, the rites and ceremonies of the law; the other, the continual history of the ancient world, and church of the Jews, which, though it be literally true, is yet pregnant with a perpetual allegory and shadow of the work of the redemption to follow. The same promise or evangel was more clearly revealed and declared by the prophets, and then by the Son Himself, and lastly by the Holy Ghost, which illumines the Church to the end of the world.

14. That in the fullness of time, according to the promise and oath, of a chosen lineage descended the blessed seed of the woman, Jesus Christ, the only begotten Son of God and Saviour of the world; who was conceived by the power and overshadowing of the Holy Ghost, and took flesh of the Virgin Mary; that the Word not only took flesh, or was joined to flesh, but was made flesh, though without confusion of substance or nature; so that the eternal Son of God and the ever blessed Son of Mary was one person; one person in such a way that the blessed Virgin may be truly and, according to the catholic faith, called Deipara, the Mother of God; one in such a way that there is no unity in universal nature, not even that of the soul and body of man, so perfect; for the three heavenly unities, whereof that is the second, exceed all natural unities; That is to say, the unity of three persons in Godhead; the unity of God and man in Christ; and the unity of Christ and the Church: the Holy Ghost being the worker of both these latter unities; for by the

Holy Ghost was Christ incarnate and quickened in flesh, and by the Holy Ghost is man regenerate and quickened in spirit.

15. That Jesus, the Lord, became in the flesh a sacrificer, and a sacrifice for sin; a satisfaction and price to the justice of God; worthy of glory and the kingdom; a pattern of all righteousness; a preacher of the word which He Himself was; a fulfiller of the ceremonies; a corner-stone to remove the separation between Jew and Gentile; an intercessor for the Church; a Lord of nature in His miracles; a conqueror of death and the power of darkness in His resurrection; and that He fulfilled the whole counsel of God, performing all the sacred offices of His anointing on earth, accomplished the whole work of the redemption and restitution of man to a state superior to the angels, to which the state of man by creation was inferior, and reconciled and established all things according to the eternal will of the Father.

16. That in time, Jesus the Lord was born in the days of Herod, and suffered under the government of Pontius Pilate, deputy of the Romans, and under the high priesthood of Caiaphas, and was betrayed by Judas, one of the twelve apostles, and was crucified at Jerusalem; and after a true and natural death, His body being laid in the sepulchre, the third day He raised Himself from the bonds of death, and arose and showed Himself to many chosen witnesses, during the period of several days; and at the end of those days, in the sight of many, ascended into heaven; where He continues His intercession; and shall from thence at the day appointed, come in greatest glory to judge the world.

17. That the sufferings and merits of Christ are sufficient to take away the sins of the whole world, but are effectual only to those who are regenerated by the Holy Ghost; who breathes His pure grace where He wills; which grace, as a seed incorruptible, quickens the spirit of man, and conceives him anew a son of God and member of Christ; so that Christ having man's flesh, and man having Christ's spirit, there is an open passage and mutual imputation; whereby sin and wrath was conveyed from man to Christ, and merit and life is conveyed from Christ to

man; which seed of the Holy Ghost first forms in us the image of Christ slain or crucified, through a living faith; and then renews in us the image of God in holiness and charity; though both works are accomplished imperfectly, and in very varied degrees even in God's elect, as much with regard to the fire of the Spirit, as to its power of illumination; which can be more or less in a large proportion; as, for example, in the Church before Christ; which, nevertheless, was partaker of one and the same salvation with us, and of one and the same means of salvation with us.

18. That the work of the Spirit, though it be not tied to any means in heaven or earth, yet it is ordinarily dispensed by the preaching of the Word, the administration of the Sacraments, the covenants of the fatners upon the children, prayer, reading, the censures of the Church, the society of the godly, the cross and afflictions, God's benefits, His judgments upon others, miracles, the contemplation of His creatures; all which, though some are more principal, God uses as means for the calling and conversion of His elect; not derogating from His power to call immediately by His grace, and at all hours and moments of the day, that is, of man's life, according to His good pleasure.

19. That the Word of God, whereby His will is revealed, continued in revelation and tradition until Moses; and that the Scriptures were from Moses' time to the time of the apostles and evangelists; in whose age after the coming of the Holy Ghost, the Teacher of all truth, the book of the Scriptures was shut and closed, so as not to receive any new addition; and that the Church has no power over the Scriptures to teach or command anything contrary to the written Word, but is as the ark, in which the tables of the first testament were kept and preserved; that is to say, to the Church has been committed only the custody and handing on of the Scriptures, together with the interpretation of them, but such only as is conceived from themselves.

20. That there is a universal or catholic Church of God, dispersed over the face of the earth, which is Christ's Spouse, and

Christ's Body; being gathered of the Fathers of the old world of the church of the Jews, of the spirits of the faithful departed, and the spirits of the faithful militant, and of the names yet to be born, which are already written in the book of life. That there is also a visible Church, marked by the outward works of God's covenant, and the receiving of the holy doctrine, with the use of the mysteries of God, and the invocation and sanctification of His holy name. That there is also a holy succession in the prophets of the New Testament and Fathers of the Church, from the time of the apostles and disciples who saw our Saviour in the flesh, until the consummation of the work of the ministry; which persons are called from God by gift, or inward anointing; and the vocation of God followed by an outward calling and ordination of the Church.

21. I believe, that the souls of such as die in the Lord are blessed, and rest from their labours, and enjoy the sight of God, yet in such a way that they are in expectation of a further revelation of their glory in the last day. At which time all of human flesh shall arise and be changed, and shall appear and receive from Jesus Christ His eternal judgment; and the glory of the saints shall then be full, and the kingdom shall be given up to God the Father; from which time all things shall continue for ever in that being and state, which then they shall receive. Thus there are three times, if they may be called so, or parts of eternity; the first, the time before beginnings, when the Godhead was alone, without the being of any creature; the second, the time of the mystery which continues from the creation to the dissolution of the world; and the third, the time of the revelation of the sons of God; which time is the last, and is everlasting without change.

F

Calvinistic Tradition and Literature

Writers of the reformed tradition whatever their language or country might be, freely acknowledged that literature can be pursued simply for the sake of the pleasure and inspiration it affords in itself. At the same time, they were able to use their artistic skill to give more worthy and exact expression both to the doctrines of the Christian faith, and to the devotion and resolution of their own hearts and wills in response to the grace of God. In this way the Calvinistic tradition in France was gradually enriched in the years after the Reformation by such poets as Théodore-Agrippa d'Aubigné (1551–1630), Jean de Sponde (1557–95), Jean Ogier de Gombauld (1580–1666). In England, it was John Milton (1608–74), influenced by the Reformed theologians William Ames (1576–1633) and Johan Wollebius (1586–1629), who gave the clearest expression in literature to the doctrines emphasized by Calvin. Calvin's teaching on justification and regeneration, through ingrafting into Christ as the second Adam and the head of the new humanity, is finely expressed in the following passage, from Paradise Lost *(Book III), in which the Father addresses the Son. The sonnet, 'On His Blindness', is an example of how the Christian should patiently bear the cross in self-denial. That on the massacre of the reformed Christians in Piedmont, carried out by the Duke of Savoy in 1665, expresses a truly Calvinistic oecumenical concern over the affairs of Church and State throughout the world. This poem helped to inspire, not only generous financial relief for the sufferers, but also also the forceful action which stopped the persecution.*

From *PARADISE LOST*

> O thou in heav'n and earth the only peace
> Found out for mankind under wrath, O thou
> My sole complacence! well thou know'st how dear
> To me are all my works, nor man the least
> Though last created, that for him I spare
> Thee from my bosom and right hand, to save,
> By losing thee awhile, the whole race lost.

D'AUBIGNÉ

Thou therefore whom thou only canst redeem
Their nature also to thy nature join;
And be thyself man among men on earth,
Made flesh, when time shall be, of virgin seed
By wondrous birth: be thou in Adam's room
The head of all mankind, though Adam's son.
As in him perish all men, so in thee,
As from a second root, shall be restored,
As many as are restored, without thee none.
His crime makes guilty all his sons; thy merit
Imputed shall absolve them who renounce
Their own both righteous and unrighteous deeds,
And live in thee transplanted, and from thee
Receive new life. So man, as is most just,
Shall satisfy for man, be judged and die;
And dying rise, and rising with him raise
His brethren, ransom'd with his own dear life.
So heav'nly love shall outdo hellish hate
Giving to death, and dying to redeem;
So dearly to redeem what hellish hate
So easily destroy'd, and still destroys
In those who, when they may, accept not grace.
Nor shalt thou by descending to assume
Man's nature lessen or degrade thine own.
Because thou hast, though throned in highest bliss
Equal to God, and equally enjoying
God-like fruition, quitted all to save
A world from utter loss, and hast been found
By merit more than birthright Son of God,
Found worthiest to be so by being good,
Far more than great or high; because in thee
Love hath abounded more than glory abounds;
Therefore thy humiliation shall exalt
With thee thy manhood also to this throne;
Here shalt thou sit incarnate, here shalt reign
Both God and Man, Son both of God and Man,

Anointed universal king; all power
I give thee, reign for ever, and assume
Thy merits; under thee as head supreme
Thrones, Princedoms, Powers, Dominions, I reduce:
All knees to thee shall bow. . . .

ON HIS BLINDNESS

When I consider how my light is spent
　Ere half my days, in this dark world and wide,
　And that one talent which is death to hide,
　Lodg'd with me useless, though my soul more bent
To serve therewith my Maker, and present
　My true account, lest he returning chide,
　Doth God exact day-labour, light denied?
　I fondly ask: But patience, to prevent
That murmur, soon replies, God doth not need
　Either man's work or his own gifts; who best
　Bear his mild yoke, they serve him best; his state
Is kingly; thousands at his bidding speed,
　And post o'er land and ocean without rest;
　They also serve who only stand and wait.

ON THE LATE MASSACRE IN PIEDMONT

Avenge, O Lord! thy slaughter'd saints, whose bones
　Lie scatter'd on the Alpine mountains cold;
　Ev'n them who kept thy truth so pure of old,
　When all our fathers worshipt stocks and stones,
Forget not: in thy book record their groans
　Who were thy sheep, and in their ancient fold
　Slain by the bloody Piedmontese, that roll'd
　Mother with infant down the rocks. Their moans
The vales redoubled to the hills, and they
　To Heav'n. Their martyr'd blood and ashes sow
　O'er all the Italian fields, where still doth sway
The triple tyrant; that from these may grow
　A hundred fold, who, having learn'd thy way,
　Early may fly the Babylonian woe.

Communities of the Elect

Presbyterian communities of Calvinistic origin, highly organized, regarding as a temporal blessing the rigorous discipline they impose on themselves, and consisting only of devoted members united among themselves by the practice of discreet asceticism, have a tendency to regard themselves as companies of elect people, who, as a result of their original sin, have been exiled into the midst of groups of impure and profane Gentiles with whom they must carefully avoid entering into too close a relationship in case it should hinder the progress of their sanctification. Thus it comes about that Calvin's disciples actually break the explicit instructions of their master, and find pleasure in the doubtful luxury of a kind of religious segregation which has at times been wrongly encouraged by their ministers. This extract from a sermon of Charles Drelincourt (1595–1669), a famous minister of Charenton, casts a revealing light on the features of the Protestant, who, on the basis of precise texts from the Bible, repudiates and fears the social pleasures of the age, and, in order the better to shield himself from all sacrilegious temptation, looks on himself as a stranger in the world.

Firstly, we recognize Strangers by their speech, as was said to St Peter, 'Thou art a Galilean, for thy speech bewrayeth thee.' In the same way it is by their speech that we recognize the Citizens of Heaven who are strangers and pilgrims on the earth. For, to use the words of the prophet, they speak in the language of Canaan, which is to say the language peculiar to the people of God. Their speech is with grace, seasoned with the salt of piety and edifying those who hear them. And just as those who are born from the earth speak as though born from the earth, so those who have heaven as their birth-place speak like heavenly people. Their most frequent utterances are psalms, hymns and spiritual songs.

Secondly, we recognize Strangers by their dress. This, too, is a way of recognizing the Citizens of Heaven. For they are clothed with light and decked with saintliness. They are like the woman clothed with the sun, having the moon under her feet, and upon her head a crown of twelve stars.

Thirdly, Strangers coming from the same town like to mix with each other and are usually seen together. Thus the Citizens of Heaven have no pleasure in consorting with the people of the world, and, as far as they can, they avoid dealings with harmful and ungodly people, for they know that bad company can corrupt good habits. But they delight in the company of good people, and seek fellowship with those who fear God and meditate on His Name. They say with the Prophet-King: 'O Lord, my goodness extendeth not to Thee, but to the saints that are in the earth, and to the excellent, in whom is all my delight.'

As a rule the Strangers are hated and ill-treated. In the same way the Citizens of Heaven are exposed to the hatred and persecution of the world. This is what our Lord wished to teach us in these divine words: 'If ye were of the world, the world would love its own: but because ye are not of the world, but I have chosen you out of the world, therefore the world hateth you.' And this is what prompts an early writer to say: 'The Church is not taken aback by her circumstances. She knows that she is a stranger in the world, and that it is the usual thing to find enemies amongst the Strangers; but otherwise her origin, her dwelling place, her hope, her grace and her dignity are in Heaven.'

The Strangers are not very fond of the land in which they are ill-used, and they speak of it only with scorn. Thus the Strangers love not the world nor the things which are in the world. And after beholding all the works that are done under the sun, they cry with the preacher: 'Vanity of vanities, all is vanity and vexation of spirit.'

The Strangers journeying along their road, do not worry unduly about the treatment they receive there. If they are comfortably put up at an inn, they do not refuse the accommodation; if they are less well done by, they patiently bear the discomforts. So it is with the Citizens of Heaven. If it pleases God to give them any blessing in the world, they rejoice in it with thanksgiving, but if they are afflicted they possess their souls in patience saying with St Paul: 'I have learned, in whatsoever state I am, therewith to be content. I know both how to be abased, and

The Temple, Charenton

how to abound: everywhere, and in all things, I am instructed both to be full and to be hungry, both to abound and to suffer need. I can do all things through Christ who strengtheneth me.'

The Strangers do not settle down in the land through which they pass. They build neither on the great highways nor in the hostelries. In the same way the Citizens of Heaven do not cling to the world nor set their hopes on things here below. They possess everything in possessing nothing, and in regarding the world as a passing phase.

The Strangers who come from some rich and fruitful country speak of nothing but this wealth and plenty, and they entertain their friends with this topic. Thus the Citizens of Heaven take pleasure in speaking of the treasures and delights of Paradise, and in conversing amongst themselves about the glory and the joy with which God crowns all who dwell therein.

The hearts of the Strangers who come from a beautiful and pleasant country are always there. Thus the Citizens of Heaven have set their affection on heaven, and they meditate upon it day and night. Like the old patriarchs, they seek their true country, that is to say a celestial one; and their appearance is like that of people who are ascending to the Jerusalem that is on high.

The Strangers who are merely passing through a country make do with only the things which are necessary for their journey. They do not burden themselves with treasures, and lay up no great store of food. In the same way, the Citizens of Heaven lay not up for themselves treasures upon earth, but rather send on their treasures to heaven, and out of iniquitous riches they make friends, so that when they fail, they may receive them into the eternal tabernacles. They content themselves with their present possessions, and say with St Paul: 'We brought nothing into the world, and it is certain that we can carry nothing out, but having food and raiment, let us be therewith content.'

Finally, we recognize the Strangers by their customs and their conversation. For they are not used to the ways of the natives of the land, and always have their own peculiarities. This is the surest sign by which we may recognize the Citizens of Heaven. For they are not conformed to this present age, but like strangers and pilgrims they abstain from fleshly lusts which war against the soul. They appear like so many beautiful stars amidst the darkness of this age, and shine as lights in the world, in the midst of a crooked and perverse nation.[118]

Charles Drenlincourt

A conventicle in the Cévennes (18th Century)

Prophetic Inspiration

The consciousness of being elected and the urge for complete separation which under certain circumstances inspired the faithful in the Presbyterian communities of the Calvinistic tradition, could give encouragement, when they were undergoing the violent effects of tyrannical civil power, to the appearance of ecstatic phenomena, the uncontrolled nature of which would without the shadow of a doubt, have filled John Calvin with powerful feelings of revulsion. To the Protestants of the Cévennes, the consequences of the revocation of the Edict of Nantes were intolerable, and the brutal treatment they suffered at the hand of barbarous ruffians made them rise in rebellion. Their ministers, whose recognized office it was to give them guidance, tried to confine them within the bounds of a strict and sober interpretation of the Scriptures. But they could not prevent the persecuted people, demented by suffering, from being

171

AVERTISSEMENS
PROPHETIQUES
D'ELIE MARION,
L'UN
DES CHEFS DES PROTESTANS,
qui avoient pris les Armes
DANS
LES CEVENNES;
ou,
DISCOURS
PRONONCEZ PAR SA BOUCHE,
SOUS L'OPERATION DE L'ESPRIT;
ET
Fidélement reçûs dans le temps qu'il parloit.

*Or à Minuit il se fit un Cri, disant, Voici l'Epoux vient;
Sortez au devant de Lui.* Matth. 25. 6.

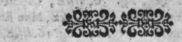

A LONDRES;
Chez ROBERT ROGER, dans les *Black-Fryars*, prés
de *Holland-Street.*

M. DCCVII.

powerfully affected by certain extravagant and spectacular charis-
matic phenomena which cast a spell over them. Their congregations
became schools of seers. They treated with distrustful respect those
who normally had oversight of them, and at the same time preferred
to follow the counsel obtained for them by a multitude of prophets
of all ages and both sexes who sprang up and prophesied. In every
possible way, attempts were made to discredit those fools of the
Lord, and to prove that they were the vehicles and playthings of
unclean spirits. They retaliated. They referred to their inward
experiences which, they proclaimed, were orthodox. They boasted
about the sublime effects of these. One of the most renowned of these
prophets of the Cévennes, Élie Marion (b. 1678), was not afraid to
compose and publish with proud humility the following apology for
himself.

It is through our inspirations that it has been put in our
hearts to leave our kindred and all that was most dear to us in the
world in order to follow Jesus Christ and to make war on Satan
and his company. It is these experiences which have given our
truly inspired ones their zeal for God and for pure religion, their
horror of idolatry and impiety, the spirit of unity, of charity, of
reconciliation and brotherly love, which reigned among us, and
their contempt for the vanities of the age and unrighteous
mammon, for the Spirit forbade looting and our soldiers sometimes reduced to ashes what treasures they found, including the
gold and silver of the temples of the idols, without trying to take
advantage of the opportunity. Our duty was to destroy the
enemies of God, not to grow rich on their spoils. And on
different occasions our persecutors proved that it was equally
impossible to tempt us with the promises they made of worldly
privileges.

It was because of these inspirations alone and the reiteration
of the orders which came this way, that we began our holy war.
How could a small number of ordinary young people without
education or experience have accomplished so much if they had
not had the help of Heaven? We had neither strength nor
counsel, but our inspirations were our refuge and support.

le page, Prophetic Warnings of Elie Marion, etc., *London, 1707*   173

Through them alone our leaders were elected and given guidance. Such inspirations have been military discipline to us. They taught us to endure on our knees the first fire of our enemies, and to attack them singing psalms to strike terror in their souls. They have transformed our lambs into lions and have caused them to perform glorious deeds. And when it happened that any of our brothers shed their blood, whether on the battlefield or as martyrs, we did not mourn for them. Our inspirations allowed us to weep only for our sins and for the desolation of Jerusalem. And I do not hesitate to state here that when God in His mercy took away my mother, He commanded me to wipe away my tears and assured me that she was at rest in His bosom. . . .

Our heaviest crosses were but light burdens to us because this intimate communion which God permitted us to have with Him relieved and comforted us. It was our assurance and our joy. . . .

If the inspirations of the Holy Spirit brought us victories over our enemies, they brought even more glorious triumph to our martyrs on the scaffold. There the Almighty did great things. There was the terrible melting-pot where the sincerity and fidelity of these inspired saints was put to the test. The wonderful words of comfort and the songs of rejoicing of the great band of blessed martyrs, even when their bones had been broken on the wheel, or the flames had already devoured their flesh, were certainly a powerful witness that their inspirations came down from the Author of every perfect gift.

I shall not forget another indubitable proof of the holiness of the inspirations with which it has pleased God to honour us. On countless occasions certain things have been precisely made known to us, with very exact details; when orders had been issued accordingly everything happened exactly as we had been told and succeeded according to the truth of the divine warning.

To God be glory and praise evermore. Amen.[119]

The Evolution of Scholasticism

The Protestant Churches of the Calvinistic tradition, though drawing their inspiration from Calvin, seem to have found that certain peculiarities of his genius had a cramping effect in their efforts to fulfil their task of teaching. Calvin was averse to breaking down theological problems into isolated questions. He always tried to show, through the use of synthetic phrases, how many different aspects one and the same question of controversy could assume. But such a method cuts across the usual practice of teaching Christian doctrine, which, in concession to certain mediaeval prejudices, seeks to proceed by the gradually developing interpretation of carefully constructed aphorisms. In the works of Calvin such concise statements as will meet this scholastic demand for a forced and gratuitous explanation cannot be found. Thus, from the end of the sixteenth century, some of the most zealous doctors of the Church set themselves to the task of reducing his teaching, at the cost of violating its method and spirit, to a series of commonplaces, skilfully arranged and gratifying to the pride of readers in theology who wished to become masters of their subject. In this way they worked out a dry and precise Calvinistic Scholasticism which reached its climax at the beginning of the eighteenth century (1713) in a collection of a hundred aphorisms drawn up by the pastor Charles Icard (1636–1715). It is a kind of summary of Calvin's teaching, and though the systematic spirit of it may be deplored, we at least can question neither its general accuracy, nor its beauty, nor its usefulness. I have reproduced some of these propositions. Those who wish information will find that they cast some light on the stark classical form of a certain type of Calvinistic orthodoxy.

1. The true wisdom of man consists in the knowledge of God the Creator and Redeemer.

10. In the government of all things the nature of God is manifested. Now His government is, in one respect, universal, by which He directs all the creatures according to the properties which He bestowed on each when He created them.

· 11. In another respect, it is special; which appears in regard to contingent events, so that if any person is visited either by adversity or by prosperity, he ought to ascribe it wholly to God; and with respect to those things which act according to a fixed law of nature, though their peculiar properties were naturally bestowed on them, still they exert their power only so far as they are directed by the immediate hand of God.

12. It is viewed also with respect to time, past and future. Past, that we may learn that all things happen by the appointment of God, who acts either by means, or without means, or contrary to means; so that everything which happens yields good to the godly and evil to the wicked. Future, to which belong human deliberations, and which shows that we ought to employ lawful means; since that Providence on which we rely furnishes its own means.

13. Lastly, by attending to the advantage which the godly derive from it. For we know certainly, (a) that God takes care of the whole human race, but especially of His Church; (b) that God governs all things by His will, and regulates them by His wisdom; (c) that He has most abundant power of doing good, for in His hand are heaven and earth, and all creatures are subject to His sway. The godly rest on His protection, see the power of hell restrained by His authority, and are persuaded that nothing happens by chance, though the causes may be concealed, but by the will of God; by His secret will which we are unable to explore, but adore with reverence, and by His will which is conveyed to us in the Law and in the Gospel.

14. The knowledge of God the Redeemer is obtained from the fall of man, and from the material cause of redemption.

15. In the fall of man, we must consider what he ought to be, and what he may be.

16. For he was created after the image of God: that is, he was made a partaker of the divine wisdom, righteousness, and holiness, and being thus perfect in soul and in body, was bound to render to God a perfect obedience to His commandments.

17. The immediate causes of the fall were: Satan, the Serpent, Eve, the forbidden fruit. The remote causes were: unbelief, ambition, ingratitude, obstinacy. Hence followed the obliteration of the image of God in man, who became unbelieving, unrighteous, liable to death.

18. We must now see what he may be, in respect both of soul and of body. The understanding of the soul in divine things, that is, in the knowledge and true worship of God, is blinder than a mole; good works it can neither contrive nor desire nor perform. In human affairs, as in the liberal and mechanical arts, it is exceedingly blind and variable. Now the will as far as divine things are concerned, chooses only what is evil. As far as lower and human affairs are concerned, it is uncertain, wandering, and not wholly at its own disposal.

19. The body follows the depraved appetites of the soul, is liable to many infirmities, and at length to death.

20. Hence it follows that redemption for ruined man must be sought through Christ the Mediator; because the first adoption of a chosen people, the preservation of the Church, her deliverance from dangers, her recovery after dispersions, and the hope of the godly, always depended on the grace of the Mediator. Accordingly, the law was given, that it might keep their minds in suspense till the coming of Christ; which is evident from the history of a gracious covenant frequently repeated, from ceremonies, sacrifices, and washing, from the end of adoption and from the law of the priesthood.

21. The material cause of redemption is Christ, in whom we must consider three things: (a) how He is presented to men; (b) how He is received; (c) how men are retained in His fellowship.

22. Christ is presented to men by the Law and by the Gospel.

23. The Law is threefold: ceremonial, judicial, moral. The use of the ceremonial law is repealed, its effect is perpetual. The judicial or political law was peculiar to the Jews, and has been set aside, while that universal justice which is described in the moral law remains. The latter, or moral law, the object of which is to cherish and maintain godliness and righteousness, is perpetual, and is incumbent on all.

24. The use of the moral law is threefold. The first use shows our weakness, unrighteousness, and condemnation; not that we

may despair, but that we may flee to Christ. The second is, that those who are not moved by promises, may be urged by the terror of threatenings. The third is, that we may know what is the will of God; that we may consider it in order to obey it; that our minds may be strengthened for that purpose; and that we may be kept from falling.

37. We have said that Christ is presented to us by the Gospel. And, first, the agreement between the Gospel, or the New Testament, and the Old Testament is demonstrated: (*a*) because the godly, under both dispensations, have had the same hope of immortality; (*b*) they have had the same covenant, founded not on the works of men, but on the mercy of God; (*c*) they have had the same Mediator between God and men—Christ.

38. Next, five points of difference between the two dispensations are pointed out: (*a*) under the Law, the heavenly inheritance was held out to them under earthly blessings, but under the Gospel our minds are led directly to meditate upon it; (*b*) the Old Testament, by means of figures, presented the image only, while the reality was absent, but the New Testament exhibits the present truth; (*c*) the former, in respect of the Law, was the ministry of condemnation and death, the latter, of righteousness and life; (*d*) the former is connected with bondage, which begets fear in the mind, the latter is connected with freedom, which produces confidence; (*e*) the word has been confined to the single nation of the Jews; but now it is preached to all nations.

39. The sum of evangelical doctrine is, to teach: (*a*) what Christ is; (*b*) why He was sent; (*c*) in what manner He accomplished the work of redemption.

40. Christ is God and man: God, that He may bestow on His people righteousness, sanctification, and redemption; Man, because He had to pay the debt of man.

41. He was sent to perform the office (*a*) of a Prophet, by preaching the truth, by fulfilling the prophecies, and by teaching and doing the will of His Father; (*b*) of a King, by governing the whole Church and every member of it, and by defending His

people from every kind of adversaries; (c) of a Priest, by offering His body as a sacrifice for sins, by reconciling God to us through His obedience, and by perpetual intercession for His people to the Father.

42. He performed the office of a Redeemer by dying for our sins, by rising again for our justification, by opening heaven to us through His ascension, by sitting at the right hand of the Father whence He will come to judge the quick and the dead; and, therefore, He procured for us the grace of God and salvation.

43. We receive Christ the Redeemer by the power of the Holy Spirit, who unites us to Christ, and, therefore, He is called the Spirit of sanctification and adoption, the earnest and seal of our salvation, water, oil, a fountain, fire, the hand of God.

44. Faith is the hand of the soul, which receives, through the same efficacy of the Holy Spirit, Christ offered to us in the Gospel.

45. The general office of faith is, to assent to the truth of God, whenever, whatever, and in what manner soever He speaks; but its peculiar office is, to behold the will of God in Christ, His mercy, the promises of grace, for the full conviction of which the Holy Spirit enlightens our minds, and strengthens our hearts.

46. Faith, therefore, is a steady and certain knowledge of the divine kindness towards us, which is founded on a gracious promise through Christ, and is revealed to our minds and sealed in our hearts by the Holy Spirit.[120]

Calvinistic Tradition and Pietistic Moralism

It may be said that throughout the eighteenth century, Calvinistic tradition, reacting in some measure against the threat of the hardening influence of scholasticism, did not defend itself sufficiently against the friendly intrusions of a kind of pietistic moralism from which Protestant theologians of the nineteenth century, in spite of many praiseworthy attempts, never succeeded in cleansing it. This religious romanticism, in which we can recognize certain elements of quietism, is given its most sincere and moving expression in the excerpt from Germaine de Stael (1766–1817) which I have had reprinted below. Deeply impressed from her childhood by the teaching of warm-hearted pastors, men outstanding in spirituality but mediocre as theologians, it remained with her that faith, being the gift of unforeseeable grace, is the sign of an election which cannot be annulled. Faith provides an effective remedy in the midst of the contradictions of experience. It ensures for the believer an uninterrupted serenity, an irreproachable way of life, a moderate portion of happiness. Though he remains a creature of time, it will assure him that he has risen above the affairs of this life to such an extent that, as he waits for a blessed eternity he neither does, nor can, nor ought to imagine any kind of makeshift salvation which will relieve him of the distaste attaching to most of his earthly routine and activity.

Religion, as it is usually understood, implies a faith that is immovable, and when this profound conviction has been received from heaven, it is adequate for life, and fills it up completely; it is in this respect that the influence of religion is truly powerful, and it is in this same respect that we ought to think of it as a gift as independent of ourselves as beauty, or genius, or any other advantage bestowed on us by Nature, and which no effort can obtain.

How would it lie in the power of the will to direct our inclinations in this regard? In matters of faith no action on ourselves is possible; thought is indivisible, we cannot detach one part of it to work upon the other: we hope or we fear, we doubt or we believe, according to the nature of our mind and the dispositions of our inborn faculties.

After having firmly established that faith is a faculty which does not depend on ourselves to acquire it, we impartially examine what it can do for our welfare and we set forth . . . its main benefits.

The imagination is the most ungovernable of the moral powers of man; its desires and its uncertainties torment him by turns. Religion opens up a long career for hope and marks out the exact route for the will; in these two respects, it gives assistance to thought. Its future is the reward of the present, everything tending to the same end, to the same degree of interest. Life becomes an inward experience, the external circumstances are only a way of giving exercise to a habitual feeling; the issue does not matter, the decision which we make is everything; and this choice, always commanded by a divine law, cannot have involved one instant of uncertainty. As soon as we are sheltered from remorse we ignore those regrets of the heart or the mind which admit the possibility of chance and judge the decision by its results. Neither successes nor their reverse bring to the conscience of the devout either satisfaction or grief. Since religious morality allows no vagueness over any of the actions of life, their decision is always simple. When the true Christian has performed his duty, his good fortune pays no more heed to it; he does not inquire what destiny is allotted to him, he does not know what is to be desired or feared, he is certain only of his duty. The better qualities of the soul, generosity, sensitiveness, far from bringing to an end all internal conflict, can in the struggle of passions, oppose one another with affections of an equal strength; but religion gives us a guide or code in which, whatever the circumstances, what we must do is determined by one rule. Everything is settled in the present, everything is indefinite in the future; at last the soul experiences a kind of well-being, it has never been more alive, but remains always calm; it is surrounded by a halo which at least gives it light in the darkness, if it is not as brilliant as the day, and this state, concealing it from misfortune, saves after all more than two-thirds of the life.[121]

Karl Barth

In opposition both to the effusions of moralistic mysticism and to the forbidding arrogance of a scholasticism which is often only too human in spite of having the appeurance of an absolute body of truth, Karl Barth has restored to the Calvinistic tradition its authentic character and method. After studying the works of Calvin with an engaging honesty, and after explaining frankly his own reactions and response, he has come to see that their central theme and their living impulse are to be found by facing up, in a divinely personal way possible to all believers, to the ever-unfolding consequences of the humanity of God in Jesus Christ. Nor does he cease to recall the whole body of the faithful, in Christian catholicity, to its two primary tasks, witness and prayer.

God's humanity and the recognition of it demand that the thought and discourse of Christian theology take up a certain attitude and be carried out in a particular way. Theology can never deal with its object in a vacuum, in mere theory. It cannot affirm, consider and express truths that rest or are moved within themselves; not an abstract truth about God, or about man, or even about the intercourse between God and man. It can never substantiate, reflect, report in a monologue. There is no such thing as a theological pictorial art. The humanity of God, just because it is an event, is not to be fixed in a picture. In correspondence with its object, the basic form of theology is prayer and sermon. It can itself only take the form of a dialogue. Its outer presupposition and motive consist in the fact that this intercourse between God and man concerns all men. What is dealt with in Him, in Jesus Christ, is the most intimate matter for all of them; what is decided is everybody's life or death. It is necessary that all should know Him, in order to have a right relation to Him, to share in Him. But many, far too many, do not yet know, or no longer know, or do not rightly know of Him. In one way or another that holds of every man. Therefore it is necessary and it is commanded that there should be proclaimed, shouted out, imparted: *tua res agitur!* Christian

Karl Barth

thought circles around both God's word of the covenant of peace, and man who has in this way or in that not rightly heard this word, to whom therefore it must be spoken. And Christian discourse is at once prayer to God and address to this man. As the exegesis of form-history has shown, it is *kerygma*, herald's call, message. That is what it is in the New Testament; and there by way of example for the whole time, following the resurrection of Jesus Christ, and preceding His direct, universal, concluding revelation. This *kerygma* does not invite or summon to any sort of freely roving speculation but to the special reflection of faith and obedience, in which man passes over from the mere 'interest' of the spectator to the genuine *inter-esse*; in which he knows his own God in the divinity of Jesus Christ and himself in His humanity—himself under God's judgment and grace, himself as recipient of His promise and His commandment; in which therefore he himself enters into the event of that intercourse with his own understanding, will and feeling. Theological thought and discourse can never bring it about that this happens to him; just on that account, it can have not only the character of address, but must also have the character of prayer. For this it can be of service to him, and it must therefore be directed to this serviceableness, corresponding to the humanity of God Himself. If this practical performance is lacking, it would mean that it was not only acting out of character, but that it was betraying its true nature, prostituting itself, and that, however 'Christian' its content might be, it would be becoming a profane thought and discourse.

The question of language, which has to be discussed with a special view to the so-called 'outsiders', is not so burningly serious as is maintained these days from various sides. For one thing, starting out again from the humanity of God, there can be no counting seriously on real 'outsiders', on a 'world that has come of age', but only with one that thinks itself of age (and daily proves that that is just what it is not). Further, if we start from here, there can only be those who have not yet conceived and apprehended themselves as 'insiders'. And again in this latter sense even the most convinced Christian must and will recognize himself anew as an 'outsider'. So then there is no need of any special language for 'insiders' and for 'outsiders'. Both are—we all are—men of the world of our time. A little bit of 'non-religious' language of the streets, of the newspaper, of literature or—at the dizziest heights—of philosophy may therefore, when the address is in question, no doubt on occasion be quite in place. But that must not in any case be a matter of special concern. A little bit of the language of Canaan, a little bit of 'revelation positivism' can also be a good thing in the address to us all, and from my experience—and in this I do not stand alone—this is, not always, but often, better understood by the most alien strangers than if one had the idea of encountering them—as 'Jesuit in Gütterli', certainly no sympathetic figure!— with any jargon that at the moment sounded 'modern'. What we have to say to them—and first to ourselves—is in any case a surprising novelty. If we see to it that it is the great novelty— the message of the eternal love of God, directed to us men, as we were, are and shall be at all times—then we shall decidedly be very well understood by them, whatever they may or may not do with it. He whose heart is with God and so really with men, can be confident that the Word of God which he is attempting to declare, will not return void.[122]

17th Century Dutch engraving from an unknown portrait. For two centuries this was the best known picture of Calvin

CHRONOLOGICAL TABLE

1483 Birth of Martin Luther
1498 Savonarola burned
1509 Birth of John Calvin
1511 Luther's journey to Rome
1517 Luther's Theses
1518 Zwingli begins his work
1520 Luther's break with Rome
1521 Luther at the Wartburg
1523 Lefèvre d'Étaples at Meaux
1524 Oecolampadius at Basle; Bucer at Strasbourg; Calvin at the College of Montaïgu
1525 Luther's marriage; Meaux group dispersed
1528 Calvin at Orleans
1529 Louis de Berquin burned
1530 Calvin at Bourges
1531 Death of Zwingli
1532 Calvin's Commentary on *De Clementia*
1553 Henry VIII breaks with Rome; Calvin's conversion
1534 The Affair of the Placards
1535 Calvin at Basle
1536 *The Institutes of the Christian Religion* in Latin; Calvin at Geneva
1538 Calvin at Strasbourg
1540 Calvin's marriage; Society of Jesus founded
1541 Calvin at Geneva; *The Institutes* in French
1545 Council of Trent opened
1546 Death of Luther; Massacre of the Vaudois of Provence
1549 The first Prayer Book
1552 Council of Trent suspended
1553 Servetus burned
1557 Triumph of Calvinistic reform in Hungary
1559 First Synod of French Reformed Churches; John Knox in Scotland
1560 Reformation in Scotland; Amboise Conspiracy
1561 The colloquy of Poissy
1562 Calvinistic reform begins in Netherlands; Council of Trent reconstituted; Massacre of Vassy
1563 End of Council of Trent

BIBLIOGRAPHY

HUGH Y. REYBURN, *John Calvin, His Life, Letters, and Work* (London, 1914).

WILLISTON WALKER, *John Calvin, The Organiser of Reformed Protestantism* (New York, 1906).

T. H. L. PARKER, *Portrait of Calvin* (London, 1954).

EMANUEL STICKELBERGER, *Calvin* (London, 1959).

JAMES MACKINNON, *Calvin and the Reformation* (London, 1936).

BASIL HALL, *John Calvin* (London, 1956).

R. N. CAREW HUNT, *Calvin* (London, 1933).

JOHN T. McNEILL, *The History and Character of Calvinism* (New York, 1954).

M. P. RAMSAY, *Calvin and Art* (Edinburgh, 1938).

WILHELM NIESEL, *The Theology of Calvin* (London, 1956).

A. MITCHELL HUNTER, *The Teaching of Calvin* (2nd edition) (London, 1954).

BELA VASADY, *The Main Traits of Calvin's Theology* (Michigan, 1951).

T. F. TORRANCE, *Calvin's Doctrine of Man* (London, 1949).

T. H. L. PARKER, *The Oracles of God* (London, 1947).
   The Doctrine of the Knowledge of God (Edinburgh, 1952).

J. F. JANSEN, *Calvin's Doctrine of the Work of Christ* (London, 1956).

H. GUISTORP, *Calvin's Doctrine of the Last Things* (London, 1955).

R. S. WALLACE, *Calvin's Doctrine of the Word and Sacrament* (Edinburgh, 1953).
   Calvin's Doctrine of the Christian Life (Edinburgh, 1959).

SELECTED WORKS OF CALVIN

The Institutes of the Christian Religion.

J. Calvini Opera Selecta. P. Barth and G. Niesel (Munich Kaiser, 1928).

Calvin's Tracts and Treatises. Ed. T. F. Torrance, 3 vols. (Eerdmans, Michigan, 1958).

Sermons on Isaiah's Prophecy. Ed. T. H. L. Parker (London, 1956).

The Deity of Christ and other Sermons. Trs. Nixon (Eerdmans, 1950).

Calvin's Commentaries and Letters. J. K. S. Reid (London, 1958).

Calvin's Theological Treatises. J. K. S. Reid (London, 1954).

Sermons on the Book of Job. Trs. Nixon (Eerdmans).

The Mystery of Godliness and Other Sermons. (Eerdmans, 1950).

REFERENCES

Abbreviations:

    C.O.   *Johannis Calvini Opera*, Brunswick, 1863–1900 (*Corpus Reformatorum*).

    I.   *The Institutes of the Christian Religion.*

1   C.O. 31: 22 (Introduction to comm. on Psalms).
2   C.O. 13: 525 (Prefatory letter to comm. on Thessalonians).
3   C.O. 31: 22 (Introduction to comm. on Psalms).
4   C.O. 5: 411–12 (Reply to Sadolet).
5   C.O. 31: 22 (Introduction to comm. on Psalms).
6   C.O. 9: 785.
7   C.O. 9: 51 (Against Westphal).
8   A. L. Heminjard: Correspondence des Réformateurs ... (Geneva 1866–97. 111/418 sq.
9   C.O. 31: 22–4 (Introduction to comm. on Psalms).
10 C.O. 5: 413 (Reply to Sadolet).
11 C.O. 5: 170–1 (Psychopannychia).
12 C.O. 31: 24 (Introduction to comm. on Psalms).
13 Institutes: Prefatory address to the King of France.
14 C.O. 31: 26 (Introduction to commentary on Psalms).
15 C.O. 31: 26 (Introduction to commentary on Psalms).
16 C.O. 10a: 5–6 (The Ordinances).
17 C.O. 9: 892 (Farewell to Ministers of Geneva).
18 C.O. 5: 438–9 (Short Treatise on Lord's Supper).
19 C.O. 31: 28 (Introduction to commentary on Psalms).
20 C.O. 5: 386–7 (Reply to Sadolet).
21 C.O. 5: 409 (Reply to Sadolet).
22 C.O. 5: 413 (Reply to Sadolet).
23 C.O. 31: 28 (Introduction to commentary on Psalms).
24 C.O. 9: 892 (Farewell to ministers of Geneva).
25 C.O. 31: 28 (Introduction to commentary on Psalms).
26 C.O. 10a: 16 (The Ordinances).

27 C.O. 6: 135 (Geneva Catechism).

28 C.O. 6: 143 and 5 (Geneva Catechism).

29 C.O. 10a: 29 (The Ordinances).

30 C.O. 7: 162 (Against the Libertines).

31 C.O. 7: 53–4 (Against the Anabaptists).

32 C.O. 7: 166 sq. (Against the Libertines).

33 C.O. 7: 164–5 (Against the Libertines).

34 C.O. 7: 150 (Against the Libertines).

35 C.O. 7: 162 (Against the Libertines).

36 C.O. 12: 65 (To the Queen of Navarre, April 1545).

37 C.O. 12: 67 (To the Queen of Navarre, April 1545).

38 C.O. 12: 67 (To the Queen of Navarre, April 1545).

39 C.O. 7: 103 (Against the Anabaptists).

40 C.O. 7:198 (Against the Libertines).

41 C.O. 7: 178–9 (Against the Libertines).

42 C.O. 7: 184 (Against the Libertines).

43 C.O. 7: 518 (Against Judicial Astrology).

44 C.O. 7: 520–1 (Against Judicial Astrology).

45 C.O. 7: 521 (Against Judicial Astrology).

46 C.O. 7: 522 (Against Judicial Astrology).

47 C.O. 7: 524 (Against Judicial Astrology).

48 C.O. 7: 537 (Against Judicial Astrology).

49 C.O. 7: 537 (Against Judicial Astrology).

50 C.O. 7: 538 (Against Judicial Astrology).

51 C.O. 7: 538 (Against Judicial Astrology).

52 C.O. 7: 538 (Against Judicial Astrology).

53 C.O. 7: 540 (Against Judicial Astrology).

54 C.O. 7: 513 (Against Judicial Astrology).

55 C.O. 7: 513 (Against Judicial Astrology).

56 C.O. 7: 514 (Against Judicial Astrology).

57 C.O. 8: 45 (On Scandals).

58 C.O. 8: 44 (On Scandals).

59 C.O. 8: 45 (On Scandals).

60 C.O. 8: 45 (On Scandals).

61 C.O. 8: 457 (Against Servetus).

62 C.O. 8: 640 (Against Servetus).

63 C.O. 8: 641 (Against Servetus).

64 C.O. 8: 641 (Against Servetus).

65 C.O. 8: 641–2 (Against Servetus).

66 C.O. 8: 643 (Against Servetus).

67 C.O. 21: 40 (Beza's Life of Calvin).

68 C.O. 21: 71 (Colladon's Life of Calvin).

69 C.O. 21: 89 (Colladon's Life of Calvin).

70 C.O. 21: 88 (Colladon's Life of Calvin).

71 C.O. 21: 109 (Colladon's Life of Calvin).

72 C.O. 21:34 (Beza's Life of Calvin).

73 C.O. 21: 39 (Beza's Life of Calvin).

74 C.O. 21: 94 (Colladon's Life of Calvin).

75 C.O. 21: 108 (Colladon's Life of Calvin).

76 C.O. 21: 117 (Colladon's Life of Calvin).

77 C.O. 11: 737–8 (To Madame de Falais, June 1544).

78 C.O. 12: 173 (To Madame de Falais, September 1545).

79 C.O. 19: 307–8 (To the Duchess of Ferrara, February 1562).

80 C.O. 16: 111–14 (To the Church of Angers, April 1556).

81 C.O. 18: 425–31 (To Admiral Coligny, April 1561).

82 C.O. 18: 344–5 (To the King of France, January 1561).

83 C.O. 19: 550 (To the Churches of Languedoc, September 1562)

84 C.O. 19: 688 (To the Countess de Roye, April 1563).

85 C.O. 20: 31 (To Monsieur de Soubise, May 1563).

86 I. Epistle to the Reader.

87 I. 1: 5: 1.

88 I. 1: 7: 5.

89 I. 4: 8: 5.

90 I. 1: 7: 4.

91 I. 2: 2: 18.

92 I. 2: 12: 1.

93   I. 2: 16: 3.

94   C.O. 50: 71 (Comm. on 2 Cor. 5: 19).

95   I. 2: 16: 3.

96   I. 2: 16: 3.

97   I. 3: 11: 10.

98   I. 3: 21: 1.

99   I. 3: 21: 1.

100   I. 3: 21: 1.

101   C.O. 47: 147 (Comm. on John 6: 40).

102   C.O. 12: 162 (Last will of Calvin).

103   C.O. 12: 163 (Last will of Calvin).

104   C.O. 9: 889 (Farewell to Seigneurs of Geneva).

105   C.O. 9: 891 (Farewell to Ministers of Geneva).

106   C.O. 9: 893 (Farewell to Ministers of Geneva).

107   C.O. 9: 893 (Farewell to Ministers of Geneva).

108   C.O. 9: 893-4 (Farewell to Ministers of Geneva).

109   C.O. 9: 894 (Farewell to Ministers of Geneva).

110   I. 4: 10: 30.

111   Karl Barth: Preface to *Textes de Calvin choisis par Charles Gagnebin* (Paris, 1948), pp. 13 and 14.

112   C.O. 13: 244-8 (To Madame de Cany, April 1549).

113   C.O. 14: 544-7 (To the five prisoners of Lyons, May 1553).

114   I. 1: 11: 12.

115   C.O. 26: 156 (Sermon on Deuteronomy 4: 15-20).

116   C.O. 1: 391.

117   *Reponse de M. Th. de Bèze aux Actes de la Conférence de Montbéliard* (Geneva, 1587), pp. 41 sq.

118   *La Bourgeoisie du Ciel* (Charenton, 1651), pp. 16 sq.

119   *Le Théâtre Sacré des Cévennes.* Ed. A. Bost (Paris, 1847), pp. 71 sq.

120   *Cent Aphorismes tirés des quatre Livres de l'Institution de la Religion chrétienne* (Brème, 1713), and Latin Version in *Calvini Institutio*. Ed. Tholuck (Berlin, 1846).

121   *De l'Influence des Passions sur le Bonheur des Individus et des Nations* Section 1, chap. 4 (1796).

122   Karl Barth: *The Humanity of God*. Excerpt in *God, Grace and Gospel*, trs. J. Strathearn Macnab (Edinburgh, 1959).

NOTE ON TRANSLATION OF TEXTS

Where the original text is in Latin, this has been translated with reference to the standard English version and to the French text.

'The Confession of Faith,' by Francis Bacon, is from the 1837 (London) edition of his works. Archaic expressions have been modernised.

NOTE ON ILLUSTRATIONS

Giraudon, pp. 30, 52, 55, 69, 154; Anderson-Giraudon, p. 147; Speiser (Basle), cover p. 3, pp. 38–39, 42–43, 45, 91, 152, 170; B.N., pp. 116, 185; *Réforme*, p. 183; Editions du Seuil, pp. 8–9, 10, 16–17, 18–19, 20, 21, 23, 25, 26, 28, 40, 45, 46, 50, 53, 64, 75, 80, 81, 83, 100, 104, 125, 137, 138, 140, 141, 151, 163; Alliance Réformée Mondiale, p. 96; E. Doumergue: *Iconographie calvinienne* (Bridel, Lausanne, 1909), pp. 6, 15, 76; *Images de passé protestant français*, cover p. 2, p. 2; Bibliothèque du Protestantisme Français (photos Seuil), pp. 59, 60, 111, 145, 148, 168, 171, 172; Collection of M. le Pasteur Bourguet (photos Seuil), pp. 114, 135, 47.

The illustrations on page 2 of the cover and the frontispiece are reproduced from the Printer's Devices of Robert Estienne and Jean Girard respectively.

Page 3 of the cover is a facsimile of the minute of the general council at which the people of Geneva adopted the Reformation, 21 May, 1536.

Mercredi vingt et sept de May / 1556

Conseil General en chapitre

CALVIN

1960 is the three hundred and fiftieth anniversary of the birth of John Calvin. This stimulating and comprehensive introduction to his life and work, by the renowned French scholar Albert-Marie Schmidt, places Calvin in his proper historical perspective as the ' second patriarch of the Protestant Reformation '. His unswerving dedication to the doctrine of individual personal salvation during a time when religious upheaval and persecution were widespread in Europe has profoundly influenced the course of present-day Protestantism. The definitive edition of his great work, THE INSTITUTES OF THE CHRISTIAN RELIGION, which he completed at considerable cost to his health, put Christian Orthodoxy on so firm a foundation that no theological controversy has since ever been able to shake it to the point of danger.

An extensive appendix of extracts from Calvin's works reveals the development of his thought; and his influence on the Protestant tradition is examined through the various other selected documents—extracts from the works of Francis Bacon, 17th-century scholastic orthodox writers, Karl Barth, and others.

For those interested in further reading, a bibliography listing the most important works by and about Calvin is appended.

63 illustrations

MEN OF WISDOM BOOKS

Muhammad	**Moses**
St Paul	
St Augustine	**George Fox**
Master Eckhart	**Buddha**
St John the Baptist	**Socrates**

MEN OF WISDOM BOOKS · MW 10

New York
HARPER
$1.50

London
LONGMANS
6/- net

Library of Congress catalog card number: 60–8972

Printed in Great Britain